Dedication

This experience is dedicated to souls HOOKED on addiction and their loved ones helping them through their journey to RECOVERY.

HOOKED On Addiction? Habitual Overuse Often Kills; Escape Dependency
Copyright © 2019 by Bruce Brummond

All rights reserved. No part of this book may be reproduced or transmitted in any form or by any means, electronic or mechanical, including photocopying, recording or set by any information storage and retrieval system, without written permission from the author except for the inclusion of brief quotations.

ISBN 978-0-978-8486-4-4
Library of Congress Control Number: 2019905545

Cover Illustration by: Nolan Harris
Cover and Interior Layout by: Fusion Creative Works

Printed in the United States of America. Lakewood, WA.

www.CharacterConstructionCompany.com

HOOKED
On Addiction?

Habitual Overuse Often Kills; Escape Dependency

Written by Bruce Brummond

(Participant) _____

(Friend) _____

This book is designed to accompany the online narrated course:
"HOOKED – Habitual Overuse Often Kills: Escape Dependency" by Bruce Brummond.
The online narrated course is available at: www.LearningCharacter.com

Recommendation

Mr. Brummond presents a unique course in education about addiction in his book titled "Hooked On Addiction?" I believe this book can be a useful tool for the "addicted," the "wonder if I am addicted" and the ever faithful "enabler."

I highly recommend this book as a study tool for not only those caught up in addiction, but also for anyone who has a **DESIRE (Ditching Evil Stuff Is Required Everyday)** to learn more about how each one of us can control our destiny.

—Jeremiah Saucier, CDP Owner/Director of Crossroads Treatment Center, Lakewood, WA.

Lila Saucier, Jeremiah Saucier and Gage are currently planning to build and operate Hope Recovery Center near Gig Harbor, Washington.

Let's look at the objectives we will be addressing in HOOKED.

- Understanding how addictions can adversely affect life's mission.
- Learn how to possibly avoid addictions and/or recover from them.
- Analyzing and altering behaviors and habits that lead to addiction.
- Practicing faith and hope to successfully bring life into balance.
- Understanding if you abuse or are addicted to harmful chemicals.
- Learning to apologize and move on while letting go of the past.
- Repairing relationships by enacting personal responsibility.
- Determining if help with addictions is needed to achieve happiness.
- Developing a desire to avoid being stuck on rock bottom.
- **HOOKED – Habitual Overuse Often Kills; Escape Dependency**.

PERSONAL MISSION

I will avoid any substance or situation

That might interfere with my ability

To share my gifts and talents

With the most possible people

In the best possible way

This experience will hopefully convince you of the value of adopting this as your PERSONAL MISSION. I will avoid any substance or situation that might interfere with my ability to share my gifts and talents with the most possible people in the best possible way!

Please write the Personal Mission in the proper order.

_____

_____

_____

_____

ADDICTIONS

Alcohol

Drugs

Food   Hobbies   Money

Greed   Relationships   Egotism

Gambling   Adrenaline   Nicotine

Sports   Control   ???????

Acclaim

Work

Analyzing Addictions

We have access to many substances and situations to give us a high that can very easily develop into addictions: Alcohol, Acclaim, Drugs, Work, Food, Hobbies, Money, Greed, Relationships, Egotism, Gambling, Adrenaline, Nicotine, Sports, Control, ?????? Can you think of others? What if we define addictions as anything that throws our life out of balance? This experience focuses on chemical addictions which are many times entangled with a variety of other dependencies.

1. Do you drink more alcohol than you feel is necessary? Would you like to limit your consumption? Is overconsumption causing problems for you and others around you? Have you tried to quit without success?

2. Would you like to limit your involvement with prescription drugs? Would you like to stop your involvement if you are involved with illegal drugs? Would you like to rid yourself of all drugs?

3. Do you eat too much, too often? Do you realize that you are eating your feelings more than eating for needed nourishment? Does your overeating lead to issues with your weight that adversely affects your overall health?

4. Do you attempt to amass possessions to help you feel better about yourself? Have you ever considered that your possessions are all about you and not about what your possessions can do for others?

5. Do you spend too much time and money trying to hit it rich? Once you start gambling it is extremely difficult, or nearly impossible to stop? Does gambling become a vehicle to develop your self-worth? Do you feel that you gamble just to gamble?

6. Do you spend too much time being involved in sports and/or watching sports? Is this creating an imbalance of how you spend your time, energy and resources?

7. Do you spend an inordinate amount of time and resources pursuing hobbies? Do you thoroughly enjoy losing yourself in fun activities? Do your hobbies adversely affect your relationships? Do they gobble up too much time and drain too many resources?

8. Are you hung up on an interpersonal relationship that interferes with other relationships? Is it difficult for you to develop balanced friendships without demanding too much control? Do you often expect way too much attention in way too many ways from your relationships?

9. Does this listing help you think about any addictions that might be creating an imbalance in your life? This experience will provide you with techniques and tools to help you balance your life; enjoy the journey!

10. Do you find yourself involved in activities to receive an adrenaline high for the risks you attempt? Do these involvements have the potential of threatening your health and longevity?

11. Do you need to be in charge? Does it always have to be your way? Do you experience difficulties in compromising with others? Would you like to learn to let go of your control? Would you like to be able to trust your ability to empower others?

12. Do you realize that you desire to have your name known by other people? Do you realize you brag too much about your accomplishments and possessions? Would you like to be known for your humility and let your accomplishments speak for themselves?

13. Do you lose yourself in working too much? Do you use productive activities as excuses to avoid social interactions with your family and friends? Do you need to be productive to ensure your feelings of self-respect?

14. Do you place your personal value on the balance in your bank account? Do you value others by the price of their possessions? Is amassing money the main goal in your life, rather than what you can do to help others with your resources?

15. Do you use nicotine products? Are you aware of the health risks of being involved with tobacco products? If you do use nicotine products...would you like to stop so you can have a chance to live longer?

16. Do you think of yourself first most of the time? Do you use these words way too often...me, myself and I? Would you like to learn the steps to help others on their journey to experience a happy life? Would you like to learn to accept others for who they are without trying to prove that you are superior to them?

17. Hopefully this listing has helped you realize that many substances and situations can adversely affect your life's balance. Do you experience any other addictions that affect your wellbeing? This methodology can help you discover how you can redirect your unwanted habits to help you find personal happiness!

18. Viewing this information with an open mind will help you gain the most from this endeavor. Hopefully this will help you balance your life so you will have a better chance of experiencing true happiness!

Our oldest grandson has a brilliant idea of how to avoid being addicted to nicotine, alcohol and drugs. He explains it very simply… "Be Smart; Don't Start!" Statistics confirm that one experience with nicotine or just one encounter with an illicit drug can begin people on a path to hook them forever. Alcohol abuse can also culminate in addiction leading to an untimely death. Please remember… "Be Smart; Don't Start!" Please share these four words with everyone you know. It is a thousand times easier to not begin an addiction than trying to stop the horrific cycle of chemical dependency!

Please place an "X" by all the correct answers to end the sentence.

The best way to avoid being addicted to nicotine, alcohol or drugs is to

Be Smart; _____

_____ Don't Start!   _____ Don't Start!   _____ Don't Start!   _____ Don't Start!
_____ Don't Start!   _____ Don't Start!   _____ Don't Start!   _____ Don't Start!

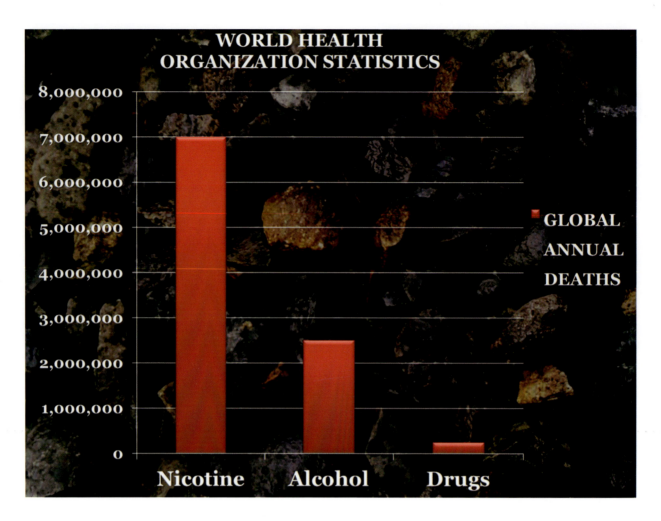

Recent statistics from the World Health Organization (WHO) indicate approximately seven million people die annually due to involvement with nicotine products. Two and a half million people succumb due to imbibing in alcohol. In addition, there are a quarter of a million deaths per year related to drug abuse. We sincerely hope this experience will help you to not become part of these shocking statistics!

Please place a "+" where you agree and a "−" where you disagree.

___ People addicted to nicotine have a very good chance of dying due to nicotine.
___ Statistics…SHAMistics…people should not believe this SHAMistic baloney.
___ Alcohol has been consumed for centuries…life's short, party hardy!
___ Legal drugs are safe to use, they are never addictive and will never hurt anyone.
___ Opioids are sensational, they are legal, take away pain, and are non-addictive.
___ When legal: nicotine, alcohol, marijuana, and opioids are never addictive.

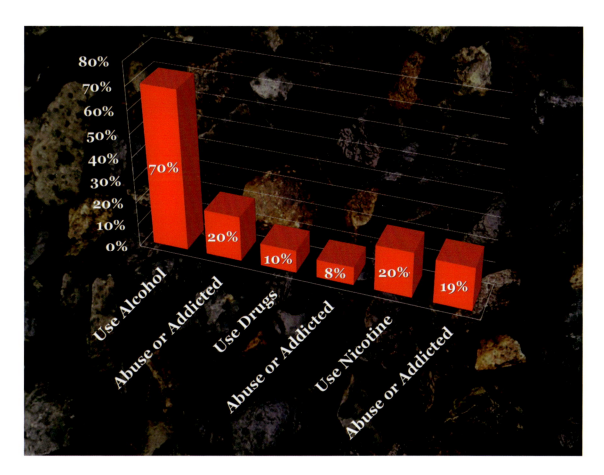

It is estimated that seventy percent of Americans consume alcoholic beverages. This results in approximately one in five Americans abusing alcohol or become alcoholics. One out of ten Americans improperly use prescription medications and/or illicit drugs on a regular basis. It is estimated that eight percent of Americans abuse or are addicted to using drugs. One in five Americans use nicotine and almost everyone who starts becomes addicted. I hope you realize that these statistical estimates, procured from a culmination of surveys, indicate the deadly consequences of being involved with alcohol, drugs, and nicotine!

Please place a "+" where you agree and a "—" where you disagree.

    ___ People who smoke nicotine products or drugs can easily stop at any time.
    ___ I enjoy smoking and I never desire to stop…it will not kill me.
    ___ I know someone who became addicted to drinking alcohol.
    ___ My friends who drink, do drugs or smoke…can all easily quit.
    ___ Addiction to alcohol, smoking and/or drugs only affects morally weak people.
    ___ Everyone should realize they are at risk for developing an addiction.
    ___ Addictions only afflict people who are born with certain inherited characteristics.

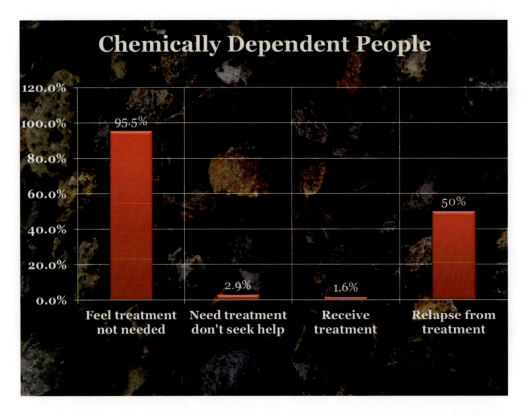

It is estimated that 95.5 % of people who are chemically dependent feel they do not need treatment. 2.9 % feel that they need treatment and don't seek help. Only 1.6 % of addicts actually participate in treatment. It is obvious to surmise from this estimate that the overwhelming majority of people who are addicted to chemical substances fail to seek treatment. Even after treatment about half relapse [some experts estimate the relapse rate is 90%.] This experience will help you take a realistic view at any issues you or someone you know might have with chemical dependency.

Please express your opinion by placing a "T" for True or an "F" for False.

___ Statistics regarding chemical dependency are difficult to accurately compile.
___ Everybody reacts differently to the same kind of drugs.
___ Just because a drug is legal doesn't necessarily indicate it's safe.
___ It is usually easier for people with addictions to get high than get treatment.
___ Most people with addictions refuse to admit they have a problem.
___ Completing treatment does not guarantee the addict will remain clean and sober.
___ Some people admit they're addicted but don't admit they need treatment.
___ Most drug addicts and alcoholics continue using to avoid withdrawals.
___ All of the above questions are true. (YES…all of the above questions are true!)

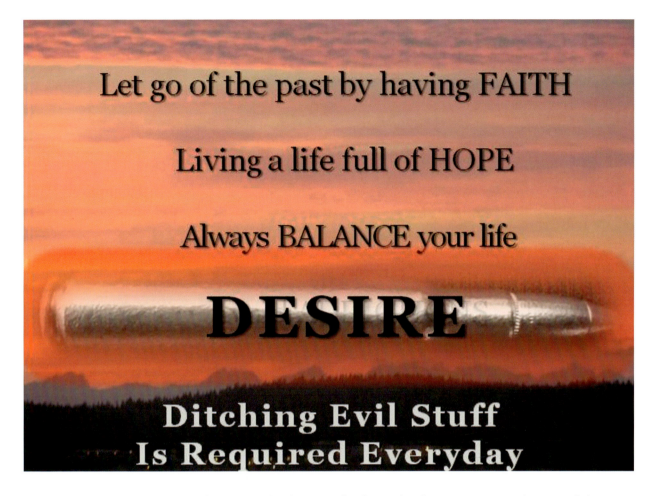

Ideally, we can let go of the past by having faith in the future. We can let go of the past by living a life full of hope. Our lives have a better chance of always being balanced if we avoid addictions. Putting a lock on the past can unlock the future by giving us freedom to experience a happy life. Would you like to lock in on a silver bullet that can improve your future? Hopefully you will display your silver bullet by enacting your **DESIRE - Ditching Evil Stuff Is Required Everyday.** Hopefully your **DESIRE** to avoid addictions will help you remain free without being imprisoned by chemical dependency!

Please place an "X" by the statements you agree with in this survey.

___ I am trying to let go of some things from my past that bother me.
___ I have a lot of faith that my future will be better than my past.
___ I have absolutely no control over what will happen in my future.
___ I believe that most people want to see me experience a happy life.
___ I am trying my best to balance my life so I can be as happy as possible.
___ I know it is up to me to display my **DESIRE** if I expect to have a better future.

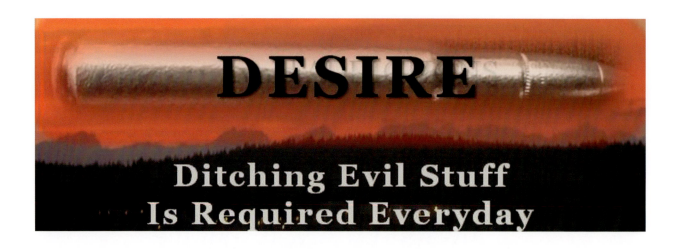

Addictions can ruin minds, bodies, dreams, relationships, careers, families and lives. It takes a tremendous amount of **DESIRE** to rid ourselves of any harmful habits. We must develop faith that evolves into hope that we can do what it takes to turn our lives away from chemical dependency.

1. Would you like to practice **FAITH - Forget All Insecurities Trust Hope?** Are you affixed to any harmful elements in your life that are holding you back from true happiness? If you want to change your future, you must be able to let go of your **PAST - Put Away Sorrowful Things!** Putting it simply…is your **DESIRE** to change any of your unwanted habits stronger than your need to stay on your current path?

2. To change our lives and reach our goals it is absolutely necessary that we have **HOPE - Harnessing Optimism Produces Empowerment.** Can you be optimistic about your ability to change any addictions to ambitions? Do you realize all the control that you possess over your life? Do you understand that it is up to you to initiate and follow through with needed changes? Would you like to become empowered in ways you never dreamed possible?

3. Would you like to **BALANCE - Boundaries And Limits Are Necessary; Careful Everybody** your life by avoiding addictions and sharing yourself with others? We can have control over our **MOOD - Managing Our Outlook Daily** if we convince ourselves we **CANDO - Control All Negativism; Develop Optimism!**

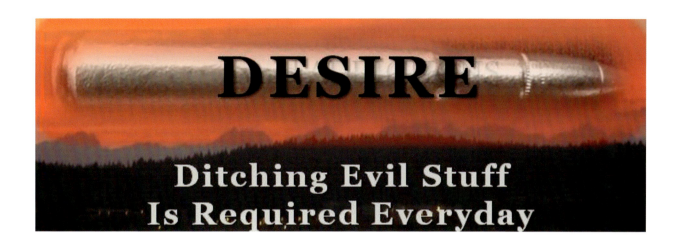

4. Are you or do you have friends or family members who are **ADDICTED?** Hopefully this definition will help people overcome their issues if **ADDICTED - Always Damages Dreams Invite Compassionate Treatment; Establish Direction!**

5. Do you possess a burning **DESIRE** to rid yourself of any addiction you might be experiencing? The silver bullet to eliminate addictions is possessing an unswerving **DESIRE-Ditching Evil Stuff Is Required Everyday!**

Summary…If you are chemically dependent would you like to succeed in your **RECOVERY?** When you…**Regain Essential Control Over Vices; Everybody Respects You.**

When your **DESIRE** leads you to a clean life you will respect yourself and others will respect you! Get ready to explore methods of balancing your life! If you are fortunate to be free of addictions this information can help you assist others with their issues.

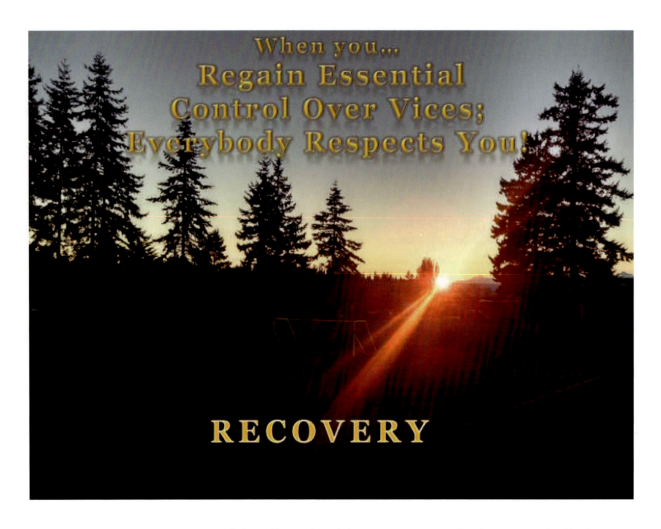

When the sun sets on your life will you be able to say you reached your goal of balancing your purpose, pleasure and peace of mind? You probably agree that most mortals have a need to perpetually readjust their balance. What if we term this struggle **RECOVERY?** When you **Regain Essential Control Over Vices; Everybody Respects You!**

Shall we view a vice as anything that throws our life out of balance? Might those vices include nicotine, alcohol, illicit drugs, gambling, food, work, power, greed and anything else that gets in our way? Hopefully you agree that changing whatever dramatically affects the balance in our lives can require a **RECOVERY!**

The first step in recovering from harmful habits is the desire to change habits that cause our lives to be out of balance.

Do you have a desire to accept the changes you might need to balance your life?

Please place a number in each space to indicate how you feel.

1 = Never   2 = Rarely   3 = Sometimes   4 = Usually   5 = Always

____ My life is perfect, I do not wish to change anything.

____ I would like to have a better chance to reach my goals.

____ My friends wish their lives were as balanced as mine.

____ I have regular habits that I would like to eliminate.

____ I have occasional habits that I would like to change.

____ Don't bother me with this baloney, I just want to enjoy my addiction(s).

____ It is up to me to take the first step to change my habit(s).

____ I know people who are currently in recovery from addiction(s).

____ I know people who would benefit by trying to recover from their addiction(s).

____ I respect people who display how they value their lives by participating in **RECOVERY**.

"You can work on your past the rest of your life. It ain't gonna get no better."

For several years I have been honored to teach the Communication FOCUS Course in many places, including jails and prisons. I always explained to the participants that I would learn much more than they would ever imagine. Here is an example… "You can work on your **PAST** the rest of your life. It ain't gonna get no better." This quote from a prison inmate very succinctly sums up our need to forget the **PAST** because…**Pages Always Stay Turned** and focus on the future. Are you able to forget trying to change your **PAST?** Are you able to use your past experiences to help you focus on what you can successfully change for your future?

Please write the words in order to spell the word PAST.

Stay   Always   Pages   Turned

_____   _____   _____   _____

Please express your opinion by filling in each blank with a "Yes" or "No."

_____ You can work on your **PAST** the rest of your life. It ain't gonna get no better.

_____ Do your **PAST** or current experiences make you feel like you are imprisoned?

_____ Would you like to tear down your walls and let happiness flood into your life?

_____ Do you spend too much time focusing on your **PAST?**

_____ Would you like to forgive yourself for things you have done to yourself and others so you can move on?

_____ One of the keys to happiness is focusing on the future by remembering that **PAST** means **Putting Away Sorrowful Things!**

_____ Be honest with yourself; if you do not possess the desire to let go of your **PAST** and improve your future, you are wasting your time and electricity on this informative activity.

_____ If you have the sincere desire to move on from your **PAST** and improve your future, you are on the right track!

Do you ever feel that your habits are imprisoning you in a deep dark hole? Would you like to be free of the feeling that the walls are collapsing in on you? Many people would like to **Celebrate Life; Escape Addictions Now!** Would you like to join my wife, Mary Ann, and Skipper on the shore admiring nature's beauty, free from all addictions? Do you have situations or substances that hold you back from having a **CLEAN** life? Would you like to experience a **CLEAN** life? If you have addictions would you like to "reboot" your life to get back to your pre-addiction peace of mind?

Most people would like to be **CLEAN - Celebrate Life; Escape Addictions Now** from anything that throws their life out of balance.

Please place the words in order to spell the word CLEAN.

Escape	Now	Celebrate	Addictions	Life
_____	_____	_____	_____	_____

Please place a number in each space to indicate how you feel.

1 = Never   2 = Rarely   3 = Sometimes   4 = Usually   5 = Always

____ I would love to be able to stand on the beach and admire the ocean without anything throwing my life out of balance.

____ I can celebrate that my life is clean of harmful situations and/or substances and I feel well balanced all the time.

____ I am involved in situations and/or substances that are not healthy for me. I know that recovery is a **Nice Opportunity**, but I have absolutely **NO** desire to change!

____ I am envious of other people's balanced lives. I am ready to do what's needed to change my habits to experience a happier life!

____ I want to **GO**: I want to take advantage of a **Great Opportunity** to live a balanced life.

Would you like to limit your consumption of **ALCOHOL - Always Limit Consumption; Often Hinders Our Lives** to remain **SOBER?** You probably agree that **Staying Off Booze Eliminates Remorse.** The term booze is a derivative of Dutch, German and English words that describe drunkenness. For thousands of years alcoholic beverages have been consumed for a variety of positive outcomes. Almost all cultures have adhered to the concept of moderation in consumption to avoid becoming overly intoxicated. Are you happy with the amount of **ALCOHOL** you consume? Does **ALCOHOL** consumption rob you of some of life's joyful experiences? Would you like to abstain from consuming **ALCOHOL** to allow you to experience all the joys you are missing because of your overconsumption of **ALCOHOL?**

Please write out the words to spell SOBER and ALCOHOL.

Eliminates	Off	Staying	Booze	Remorse
_____	_____	_____	_____	_____

Consumption	Always	Lives	Often	Our	Limit	Hinders
_____	_____	_____	_____	_____	_____	_____

Please express your feelings by filling in each blank with a "Yes" or a "No."

____ Consuming alcohol can make people **DRUNK – Didn't Realize Until Now… Klunk!**

____ I drink alcoholic beverages.

____ I seldom drink alcohol, when I do it is a very small amount.

____ On occasion, I drink more than I should.

____ I feel compelled to drink to ease the stress in my life.

____ Sometimes excessive drinking blocks my memory.

____ I drink daily. No way do I want to be sober every day.

____ I'm jealous of my friends who don't drink.

____ Alcohol has created many issues in my life.

____ I drink to forget about my drinking problems.

____ I would love to stop drinking alcohol. I need it to avoid withdrawals!

For many decades my Mother carried this one-hundred-dollar bill so she would always possess some **CASH**, she never intended to spend it. Several decades ago I inherited the cherished **CASH**. You guessed it…because we avoided addictions the money has been preserved for more than half a century.

Would you like to possess **Clean And Sober Habits** so you can have **CASH**?

Are there other habits that are costing you money? Would you like to "reboot" your life to go back to the time that you had squeaky **Clean And Sober Habits**?

Please place the words in order to spell the word CASH.

Sober   And   Habits   Clean

_____   _____   _____   _____

    Is **FOOD – Forget Overeating Observe Diet** an addiction for you? Do you consume more than you need in an effort to reduce stress and provide comfort? Do you consume alcohol or non-prescribed drugs on a regular basis? Are you regularly engaged with nicotine products?

    Please be aware: **Harmful Actions Blatantly Injure The Soul!** Would you like to cancel out all these **HABITS?** Bottom line: do you have **HABITS** that are negatively affecting your life?

Please place the words in order to spell the word HABITS.

Injure   Soul   Actions   Harmful   Blatantly   The

_____   _____   _____   _____   _____   _____

    Hopefully you would like your **HABITS** defined this way: **Happiness Advances By Isolating Temptations.** Does it look like my grandson is learning to isolate potentially habit-forming pain killers that were prescribed for his papa's shoulder surgery?

    Is it best to discard any prescription drugs that you no longer need? For the sake of everyone who may be near the drugs, regardless of their age: please discard all unneeded prescription drugs. Would you also like to isolate any of your other unwanted **HABITS?**

Please place the words in order to spell the word HABITS.

Isolating   Advances   Happiness   By   Temptations

_____   _____   _____   _____   _____

Place a number in each blank to indicate how you would end the sentence.

1 = Absolutely   2 = Usually   3 = Sometimes   4 = Rarely   5 = Never

To help me reach the peak of my dreams I have habits that I would like to _____

_____ always hide from the law because I don't like jail!
_____ eliminate as soon as possible.
_____ stop before they cause my death.
_____ have people quit lecturing me about stopping.
_____ restrict to enable me to live longer.
_____ have them become even more addictive.
_____ hide from my friends and family.
_____ have others start so I won't feel so guilty.
_____ slow down so I can develop my self-worth.
_____ be known for quitting so I can proudly display my self-worth.

Certain Habits Always Negatively Ground Everyone.

Is it possible to **CHANGE** any of your undesirable habits? Certainly!

Do you think these people are planning to clean up their dirty habits of slogging through the mud?

Please write the words in order to define negative CHANGE.

Habits   Negatively   Everyone   Always   Certain   Ground

_____   _____   _____   _____   _____   _____

Hopefully you agree that **Correct Habits Activate New Goals Effectively.**

Can we develop new patterns to clean up habits we would like to **CHANGE?** Absolutely!

Would you like to clean up anything in your life, like this beautiful couple has done?

Do you have any habits you would like to clean up so you can develop better habits?

Please write the words in order to define positive CHANGE.

Habits   New   Effectively   Activate   Correct   Goals

_____   _____   _____   _____   _____   _____

Do you have **BALANCE** in your life? As your life revolves, do the facets in your life properly align? While you are journeying through life, do you remain aware that **Boundaries And Limits Are Necessary: Careful Everybody?** Life can certainly be rocky as Skipper's Mother is finding out. However, if we notice that our boundaries and limits keep us safe, we can be empowered to proceed with caution.

Do you agree that one of life's paramount challenges is to maintain a **BALANCE** of what we do and how we do it? Would you like to shrink any of your boundaries to provide you a better feeling of wellbeing?

Please write the words in order to spell the word BALANCE.

___ ___ ___ ___ ___ ___ ___

Please place an "X" by what will help you balance your life.

My life would be more balanced if I_____

_____ drank less alcohol and/or used fewer drugs.

_____ ate less unhealthy food, fewer sweets and packaged treats.

_____ used only necessary prescription medications prescribed for me.

_____ could avoid anger and confrontations by controlling my emotions.

_____ would spend less time hiding from my family and friends.

_____ would consider the impact of what I say before I say it.

_____ and/or people near me would stop smoking cigarettes and/or using drugs.

_____ didn't have to feed my ego by perpetually seeking acclaim.

_____ didn't have to be greedy about relationships, money and possessions.

_____ would avoid gambling that ruins my finances and relationships.

_____ would get more sleep, exercise regularly and eat only healthy foods.

_____ would control what I can control and let go of things that I cannot change.

_____ refused to listen to people with poisonous attitudes who unfairly criticize me.

Many people feel that their most valuable possession is their best **FRIEND - Fabulous Relationships Inspire Empathy Not Drama.** Personal friendships and inspirational relationships give us a feeling of belonging which results in peace of mind. Some friendships evolve into long lasting relationships exemplified by these married couples. The people in this audience are celebrating the inspiration they receive from the leader of their faith community.

Please place an "X" by all statements that apply to end the following sentence.

Friends provide us_____

   ____ a feeling of wellbeing to help us balance our emotions.
   ____ help and support through our trials and tribulations.
   ____ inspiration to become the best we are capable of becoming.
   ____ someone to blame for our "missteaks" and shortcomings.
   ____ a kind ear to listen to our innermost secrets.
   ____ a shoulder to cry on when times get really tough.
   ____ a hand to hold to remind us they are always there for us.
   ____ encouragement when life gives us overwhelming challenges.
   ____ a realistic look at ourselves, whether we like it or not.
   ____ unconditional empathy whenever we need help in any way.

Are you surrounded by people you would like to emulate and others possibly you would not like to use as role models? Here is a lesson to remind us to be aware of friends who might be convincing us to put things in our mouths that might develop into bad habits.

Please place an "X" to indicate your responses to this survey.

    ___ I can list at least six people who are my positive role models.
    ___ I learn different positive things from my different role models.
    ___ Some people have tried to convince me to put something harmful in my mouth.
    ___ I have put something in my mouth that ended up causing many problems.
    ___ I have decided I will not put anything in my mouth that might harm me.
    ___ I will not try to convince anyone else to put anything harmful in their mouth.
    ___ I should remember that "peer pressure is only ear pressure not fear pressure."
    ___ I should influence others to always carefully consider what they put in their mouths.

Is it possible to view everyone we encounter as a friend who could use our **EMPATHY?** The word **EMPATHY** certainly encompasses a wide variety of meanings. Hopefully you agree that this sums up your feelings about **EMPATHY - Exercising My Personal Actions To Help You**.

Can you help others overcome elements in their lives that could potentially harm their existence? Can others help you? Can you help yourself? Do you practice displaying **EMPATHY** or simply talk about displaying **EMPATHY** for you and others?

Please place the words in order to spell the word EMPATHY.

My   Help   To   Exercising   Actions   Personal   You

_____ _____ _____ _____ _____ _____ _____

Place a number to indicate how you would like to end the following sentence.

1 = Doesn't apply   2 = Ask someone else   3 = Maybe   4 = Hopefully   5 = I'm all in

If someone needs my **EMPATHY**_____

_____ they can dream on…I have enough of my own problems!

_____ I will help them if I can make some money doing it.

_____ I will do what I can within reason to help them.

_____ I will ideally help them learn how they can help themselves.

_____ I will blame them for their situation and tell them to kiss off!

_____ they shouldn't expect help from anyone especially me!

_____ regarding any kind of addiction, I will love to help!

_____ they can count on me to help in any way possible!

_____ they are proving that they are a loser…I hate losers!

_____ to turn their lives around…I understand…been there!

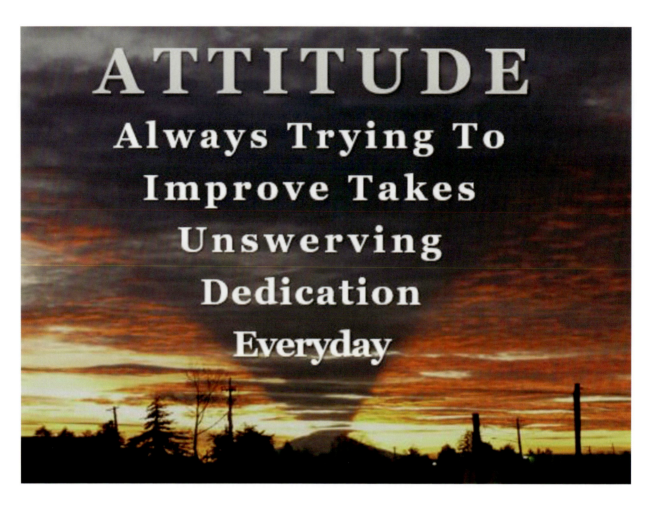

ATTITUDE - Always Trying To Improve Takes Unswerving Dedication Everyday. Do you agree that improvement from harmful habits is accomplished moment by moment? Minute by minute? Hour by hour? Day by day? Week by week? Month by month? Year by year? Decade by decade?

   Do you agree that avoiding and overcoming possible addictions is a lifetime pursuit that requires unlimited dedication every moment of every day? Do you approach each day as it's a **NEW DAY** with a new challenge to improve your **ATTITUDE?**

Write the following words in order to define ATTITUDE and NEW DAY.

To	Improve	Dedication	Everyday	Takes	Unswerving	Always	Trying
___	___	___	___	___	___	___	___

Wishes	Decisions	Enjoy	Affect	Now	You
___	___	___	___	___	___

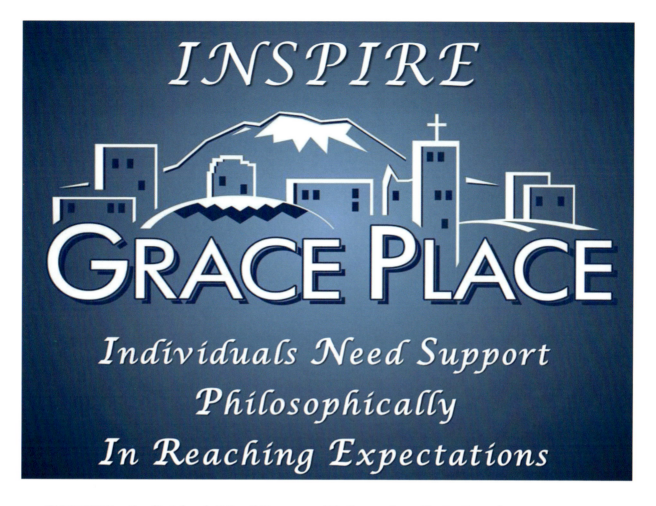

INSPIRE – Individuals Need Support Philosophically In Reaching Expectations.
Many people find inspiration by participating in faith-based organizations. Spiritual communities offer members feelings of belonging, being needed and being loved. Do you currently belong to any organization(s) of your choosing? Do you receive a feeling of belonging when you attend an organization's event?

Does it give you a feeling of being needed if you are involved in the organization's activities? Does the "icing on the cake" appear if you feel loved by the people in the inspirational organization? Would you imagine that statistics confirm that adding a Spiritual dimension to recovery greatly enhances the recovery process? You are correct… inspiration helps us avoid and/or overcome addictions!

Please write out the word INSPIRE.

Philosophically   Expectations   Need   Individuals   Support   In   Reaching

_____   _____   _____   _____   _____   _____   _____

Please place an "X" on each statement that you agree with.

1. You are inspired to belong…

    ___ If you are a member of a team, club, family, organization.

    ___ If you proclaim your allegiance to the group.

    ___ If you abide by the stipulations of membership.

2. You are inspired to feel needed…

    ___ If you share some of your time.

    ___ If you share some of your gifts.

    ___ If you share some of your talents.

3. You are inspired to feel loved…

    ___ If you have shared some of your time.

    ___ If you have shared some of your gifts.

    ___ If you have shared some of your talents.

    ___ If you have been accepted on an extraordinary emotional level.

Please sum up your feelings by filling in the blanks.

1. Do you allow yourself to be inspired by being a member of organizations?

   _____ Yes   _____ No

2. Please list the organizations where you feel you belong.

   _____   _____   _____

   _____   _____   _____

3. Please list other groups you can potentially join to seek inspiration.

   _____   _____   _____

   _____   _____   _____

   _____   _____   _____

4. Would you like to prove you are inspired by joining any organization(s)? If you wish to be inspired, you need to take the **STEP – Start To Eliminate Procrastination**.

Place an "X" by your decision regarding taking the first STEP to be inspired.

___Yes, I will take the **STEP**; I will start right now!

___ No, I do not want to belong to any organizations: I love isolation!

Let's take a closer look at how we inspire

Do I... Inspire or Irritate..Assure or Annoy..Infuriate or Influence

Am I... Depressed about Past.. Panicked about Present.. Fearful about Future

Do I share...

Goodness or Garbage

Pain or Peace

Stress or Sincerity

Do I want to be...

Helpful or Hurtful

Compassionate or Controlling

Selfish or Selfless

Let's take a closer look at how we inspire. Ask yourself some simple questions: do I Inspire or Irritate, Assure or Annoy, Infuriate or Influence? Am I Depressed about Past, Panicked about Present, Fearful about Future? Do I share Goodness or Garbage, Pain or Peace, Stress or Sincerity? Do I want to be Helpful or Hurtful, Compassionate or Controlling, Selfish or Selfless?

Do you think you inspire others? Do you understand how you might be a more positive influence on others? Do you avoid people who pull you down and soil your soul?

1 = Never   2 = Rarely   3 = Sometimes   4 = Usually   5 = Always

Please place a number in each space that best describes how you usually affect others.

_____Inspire _____Irritate _____Assure _____Annoy _____Infuriate _____Influence

Let's take a closer look at how we inspire

Do I... Inspire or Irritate..Assure or Annoy..Infuriate or Influence

Am I... Depressed about Past.. Panicked about Present.. Fearful about Future

Do I share...
Goodness or Garbage

Pain or Peace

Stress or Sincerity

Do I want to be...
Helpful or Hurtful

Compassionate or Controlling

Selfish or Selfless

1 = Never   2 = Rarely   3 = Sometimes   4 = Usually   5 = Always

Please write in a number that best answers the questions about you.

    ___ Am I depressed about my past?   ___ Am I panicked about the present?
    ___ Am I fearful about the future?   ___ Do I inspire myself and others?
    ___ Do I share goodness?   ___ Do I share garbage?
    ___ Do I share pain?   ___ Do I share peace?
    ___ Do I share stress?   ___ Do I share sincerity?

1 = Never   2 = Rarely   3 = Sometimes   4 = Usually   5 = Always

Please write in a number to describe what you want to do.

    ___ I want to share stress.   ___ I want to share sincerity.
    ___ I want to be helpful.   ___ I want to be hurtful.
    ___ I want to be compassionate.   ___ I want to be controlling.
    ___ I want to be selfish.   ___ I want to be selfless.
    ___ I want to share garbage.   ___ I want to share goodness.

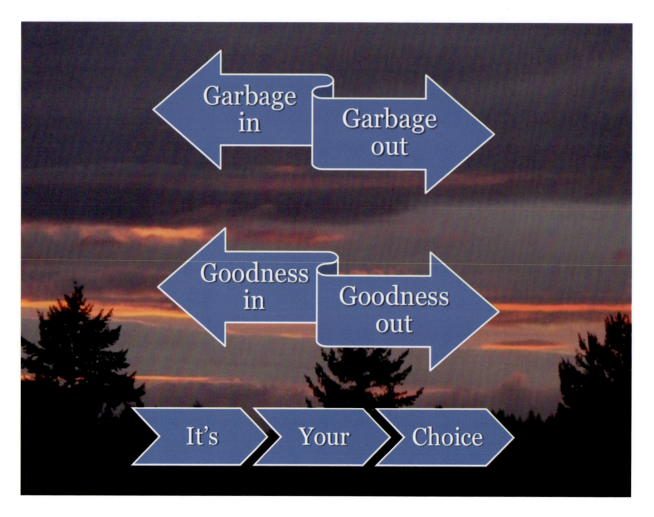

Garbage in, Garbage out, Goodness in, Goodness out…It's Your Choice. Do you think we are a product of what we allow to enter our minds and bodies? Are there things you would like to restrict from entering your body? Are there concepts that you would like to not enter your mind? Would you like to redirect the negative influences in your life so positive influences can permeate your existence? If your answer is yes to any of these: why are you waiting?

Please fill in the blanks to match the above graphic regarding garbage.

_____ _____   _____ _____

_____ _____   _____ _____

_____ _____   _____ _____

1 = No way   2 = I can't   3 = Hope to   4 = Gradually   5 = Right now

Fill in each blank with a number to respond to each statement that ends the sentence.

I will take the following actions regarding garbage and goodness_____

___ I will stop associating with people who bring their garbage into my life.
___ I will seek inspiration from organizations that share goodness.
___ I will avoid breaking the law and always tell the truth.
___ I will stop consuming alcohol and/or taking harmful drugs.
___ I will make certain I am not involved with any kind of nicotine products.
___ I will share goodness by seeking forgiveness for the bridges I have burned.
___ I will perpetually apply self-help techniques and **TOOLS – To Optimize Our Lives.**
___ I will properly nourish my mind, body and soul, plus exercise on a regular basis.
___ I will be a role model of sharing regular acts of kindness and compassion with others.
___ I will continue to blame others so I will not have to accept responsibility for my own actions.

Bountiful Love Endures Scorn'n Sadness; Enters the Deity. Millions of people throughout the world feel that being **BLESSED** helps them tackle life's overwhelming challenges. Our existence is a perpetual roller coaster of emotions while we experience good and evil…some feel that inspiration from a Higher Power can help them heal.

This is the coffee shop where four Lakewood, Washington Police Officers lost their lives during an ambush. Pastors joined together to present a blessing ceremony to rid the site of evil spirits. The ceremony seemed to help friends and families of the deceased officers find comfort. Some people seek help from a Higher Power, some don't. Do you seek inspiration from an external force? Do you feel that seeking inspiration might help you to better endure life's challenges?

Please use the above words to spell the word BLESSED.

B_____ L_____ E_____ S_____'n

S_____ E_____ t_____ D_____

44

Please place an "X" by the endings of the sentence you agree with.

Believing in a Higher Power is a personal choice.
I personally feel that_____

___ a Higher Power is simply a smoke screen to answer difficult questions.

___ believing in a Higher Power helps many people throughout their lives.

___ I don't care what people believe, don't bother me with that nonsense.

___ everybody has their own set of beliefs that they use to guide their lives.

___ I appreciate people who respect my feelings regarding a Higher Power.

___ I always display respect to the feelings of others regarding a Higher Power.

Shortly after Lakewood's horrible tragedy these pastors gathered together to mourn because they believe in the value of **PRAYER - Powerful Resources Await Your Every Request.** Dale Carnegie suggested that reciting our goals helps make those goals much more attainable.

These community leaders were enacting Mr. Carnegie's suggestion with the added possibility of help from above!

Do you often repeat your goals to remind yourself of your direction? Does positive self-talk help you, especially if you repeat it?

Please place the words in order to spell the word PRAYER.

Await   Powerful   Request   Resources   Your   Every

_____ _____ _____ _____ _____ _____

CHANGE - Certain Habits Always Negatively Ground Everyone. We had the habit of keeping fish like this beautiful Red Snapper that Dave caught in Canada many years ago. My, oh my, that fish was certainly delicious! He broke the habit of keeping fish when he started fishing for bass in lakes. He learned to turn them loose so they would grow, and he could catch them again.

He and I fished for bass in many places, including Lake Washington. What did we do with them? We let them go. He often took his friends fishing. What did they learn to do with the fish? They learned to also **LET GO.**

We all struggle with habits that impede our progress towards achieving a successful life. Are there habits that you would like to **LET GO** so **CHANGE** is possible in your life to allow you freedom to reach your goals?

Remember...Losing Every Temptation Generates Opportunities!

Do you see the small fin by Dave's index finger? That adipose fin indicates this beautiful king salmon was a native and we could not retain him. Yes, we again had to **LET GO!**

Ironically, we were right next to a fisheries patrol boat. Can you always imagine that law enforcement personnel are watching to make certain you **LET GO** of anything you should not keep? Would this encourage you to **LET GO** of anything that is not good for you to keep?

Please align the words to spell CHANGE and LET GO.

Ground	Certain	Always	Habits	Negatively	Everyone
_____	_____	_____	_____	_____	_____

Every	Temptation	Opportunities	Losing	Generates
_____	_____	_____	_____	_____

Would you like to **MOVE ON** with your life and leave any addiction issues far behind? Consider accepting this definition of **MOVE ON - Managing Our Victimization Effectively; Overcoming Neglect.** Is it easy for people with addiction issues to become imprisoned in a pity party while blaming others for turning them into a victim?

Does everyone accept the fact that their actions have created their own issues? Do people neglect the things that provide them joy because they continue thinking of themselves as a victim?

Does it look like these wonderful ladies, we met in Spain, are enjoying solid relationships that bring them joy? Would you like to move on as these happy ladies are exemplifying?

Please place the words in order to spell the words MOVE ON.

Overcoming   Neglect   Managing   Effectively   Victimization   Our

_____   _____   _____   _____   _____   _____

To achieve peace of mind it helps to be able to forget our past and **MOVE ON** – **Managing Our Victimization Effectively; Overcoming Neglect**.

Please place an "X" by the statements that help you MOVE ON.

___ I enjoy dwelling on issues of the past, it gives me an excuse for self-medication.

___ Creating drama is entertaining, I do not wish to let go and **MOVE ON**.

___ I always try to blame my problems on as many people as possible.

___ I truly enjoy having addictions control all my life, it's a blast.

___ I realize that it is up to me to avoid enabling myself to become a victim.

___ I am trying my best to let go of my past so I can prepare for a better future.

___ I really appreciate people lecturing and nagging me about my actions.

___ I appreciate people displaying they care about me by stating facts about my habits.

___ I will take the advice of caring people and do everything I can to **MOVE ON**.

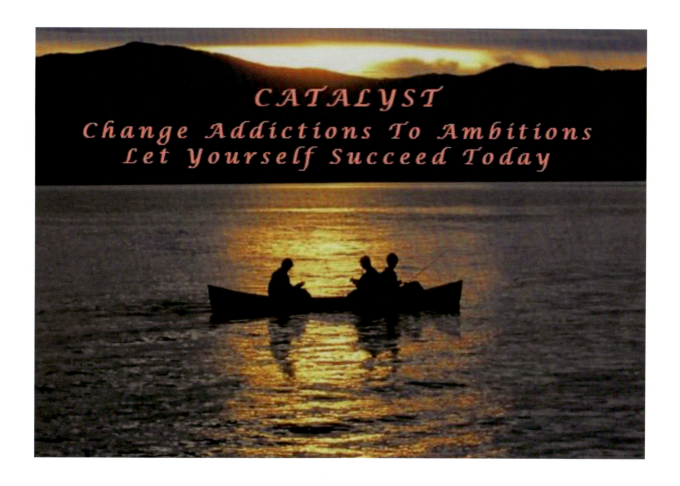

CATALYST - Change Addictions To Ambitions; Let Yourself Succeed Today. As the definition so succinctly describes working towards fulfilling our ambitions, rather than wallowing in addictions, is a recipe for success. Do you have an ambition that is yet to be fulfilled? Can you dedicate your time and effort to work towards a long-desired goal?

Do you think it has been difficult for me to cease conducting choirs after spending forty years addicted to making music? Yes, I realized making music had become an addiction, albeit a good one. What did I do to overcome my addiction to making music? I immediately immersed myself into this massive project that has consumed me for over a decade. How would you define my latest addiction? You guessed it…I'm now addicted to helping people learn to live happy lives!

Can you change any of your addictions to ambitions?

Please write the word CATALYST in the proper order.

Let   Succeed   Change   Ambitions   Today   Yourself   Addictions   To

_____ _____ _____ _____ _____ _____ _____ _____

AMBITION - Activating Meaningful Beliefs Is The Inspiration Often Needed. One of the major keys to success is to be inspired to witness our beliefs develop into actions that produce positive results. We inspire ourselves to accomplish goals and our beliefs are fulfilled when we attain our goals.

Are you a self-starter? Do you activate your desires to apply your beliefs? Does our oldest grandson look like he is displaying his **AMBITION** to begin walking? He is learning to act as a "**B Triple A Person.**" He is learning to **Be Ambitious And Accountable**.

When he falls down will he blame others or simply try to stand back up and try walking again? Is he being a role model for his younger cousin?

Are people patterning their behavior after you? Are you ambitious and accountable? Can you display your **AMBITION** one small step at a time? Hopefully you are getting ready to celebrate your baby steps!

Please place one "X" to indicate your STEP – Start To Eliminate Procrastination.

___ I am clean and sober, and I have promised myself I will stay clean and sober.

___ I will take my first step right now to be clean and sober.

To display our ambition, we need to **START - Success Takes A Realistic Try.** Is this gentleman acting as an incredible role model for his baby by experiencing an online self-improvement course? As this baby grows do you think she will be encouraged to value learning?

Do children reflect patterns of behavior from their elders? Can this be a good thing and a bad thing? What do you **START** that creates a pattern for people observing you as a role model? Would you like to change your role modeling to improve the patterns of behaviors of people observing you? Now is the time to try to **START**!

Please place the words in order to spell the word START.

Takes	A	Try	Success	Realistic
_____	_____	_____	_____	_____

I hope you will always remember that **TRY** means **To Respect Yourself.** This is a group of "special needs students" who learned to perform beautiful music with their hand bell choir. You will soon understand why I call "special needs students" simply "special students."

While serving as a school district administrator I procured hand bells for this group. The compassionate, creative director developed a color-coded note recognition system and trained one of the members how to direct the young musicians. They displayed their incredible talents throughout the area, including this performance at the Washington State Capitol Building in Olympia.

Two things were always guaranteed to happen at their performances. The youngsters' magnificent music put the audience in tears and the marvelous "special students" received a standing ovation because…they…gave…it a **TRY!**

Do you have special needs that you would like to overcome? Give it a **TRY!**

Please use three words to spell the word TRY.

Respect	Yourself	To
_____	_____	_____

The steps to rescuing relationships can be very rocky. Our efforts may be interrupted as we travel a path that will hopefully help us build and maintain long lasting relationships. If our plans fail to reach fruition, we may need to forget the past and plan for the future by offering a sincere apology. Here is a magic word that can help us find a new bridge for rebuilding relationships; **SORRY-Success Often Requires Rescinding Yourself!**

"I'm **SORRY** Skipper we can't cross this bridge. Let's try to find a new bridge." Can you tell people you are **SORRY?** Would a sincere **SORRY** and a thorough apology help you rebuild bridges to repair failed relationships? Might it be time to attempt to build some new bridges?

Please place an "X" to indicate your apology plans.

___ I will attempt to build new bridges by telling people I am **SORRY** and apologize.

___ I lead an absolutely perfect life, I do not owe anyone an apology.

___ I will tell people that I am **SORRY** and apologize whether they accept it or not.

___ I am always willing to tell people I am **SORRY** and attempt to offer an apology.

The five steps of a sincere apology

"I am sorry and I apologize because I now understand that I offended you when I said (did) _____.

I said (did) it because I was _____.

I was wrong and I should have said (done) _____.

In the future I am planning to _____ so that doesn't happen again.

I sincerely hope you accept my apology because I value our relationship more than _____."

**Use these five steps to help build bridges.
Please practice writing a sincere apology.**

1. "I am sorry, and I apologize because I now understand that I offended you when I said (did) _____
   _____.

2. I said (did) it because I was _____
   _____.

3. I was wrong and I should have said (done) _____
   _____.

4. In the future I am planning to _____
   _____so that doesn't happen again.

5. I sincerely hope you accept my apology because I value our relationship more than
   _____
   _____."

What if we view this halibut fishing trip as an example of balancing our Purpose, Pleasure and Peace of Mind? We boated a nice halibut. Our Purpose was to catch a halibut: check! We experienced a great deal of Pleasure on a beautiful day of fishing: check! The day provided us priceless Peace of Mind: check!

Can you measure everything that you do with the three P's? Try it. You will probably be amazed how this simple test provides an effective tool to help you in making decisions.

Can you relate to the magnificent feeling that we have when these three things align?

Do you think Skipper is dreaming of how delicious that fish will taste? Is there anything in your life that you would like to change to help you balance your Purpose, Pleasure and Peace of Mind?

Please place an "X" on the three Ps that lead to a balanced life.

___Pride   ___Pleasure   ___Problems   ___Purpose   ___Pressure

___Progress   ___Pretend   ___Prosperity   ___Promises   ___Planning

___Perturbed   ___Powerless   ___Perplexed   ___Patience   ___Procrastinate

___Persistence   ___Peace of Mind   ___Pain   ___Power   ___Passion

Please place an "X" in three spaces to indicate the three P's of being a person.

____ Perpetually complain until you get your way.

____ Protect your secrets so you can do anything.

____ Pleasure.

____ Procrastinate…never try…you will never fail.

____ Positiveness is for people who are insecure.

____ Purpose.

____ Put others down until you feel better.

____ Pleasantly lie to make you look smart.

____ Peace of Mind.

LIES lead to a downward spiral of more **LIES**, less trust, more **LIES**, less trust, more **LIES**, less trust, more **L-I-E-S...Losers Intentionally Exaggerate; Stop!** Most people believe that the best way to cover up a lie is to tell another lie.

How about this idea? Don't be a loser…don't exaggerate the truth until it becomes a lie! You needlessly upset many people…if you lie…Stop!!!

Is there anyone you would like to apologize to for telling **LIES**? Can you do it now?

Winners are honest. Losers enter a downward spiral of exaggerating and telling **LIES**!

Spell the word LIES by writing the definition in the correct order.

Exaggerate	Losers	Stop!	Intentionally
_____	_____	_____	_____

Do you know people who lie so much that they are in total **DENIAL?** Might they say to themselves **"Didn't Even Notice I Always Lie?"** Might some people lie so much that they have trouble separating fact from fiction? Is it easy for lying to become a habit?

Do you always ask yourself; "Is what I am saying the truth?" Can you honestly ask someone if they feel you always tell the truth? Whose responsibility is it for you to tell the truth and avoid blaming others?

List how you feel about denial by placing an "X" in the statements you agree with.

___ I face the facts of what I have done and accept responsibility for my actions.

___ I know people who are in **DENIAL** about addictions; they are lying to themselves.

___ I am honest with myself about what I need to do to experience a clean and sober life.

___ I am honest with myself about anything that may be throwing my life out of balance.

___ I feel that if I agree with someone's **DENIAL**, I help them perpetuate their lie.

___ Accepting the truth regarding addiction is absolutely essential for successful recovery.

___ **DENIAL** is a lie…is a lie…is a lie…is a lie…is a lie…is a lie…is a lie…is a lie!!!

___ When people surrender to recovery, they prove that their lie is dead!

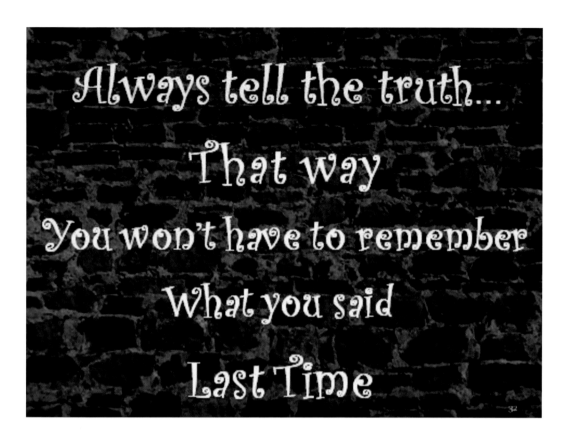

"Always tell the truth…that way you won't have to remember what you said last time!"

Thank you, Mark Twain! I have recited this quote hundreds and hundreds of times for over half a century. It is as meaningful today as it was when I began reciting it while attending high school.

What does this mean to you? Is it difficult to remember stories that we may have made up compared to actual events? Might this motivate you to tell the truth? Do you wish everyone you know would abide by this quote?

Please write in numbers 1-6 to place the Mark Twain quote in order.

_____ that way

_____ "Always tell the truth

_____ last time!"

_____ you won't

_____ what you said

_____ have to remember

Some people **BLAME** others rather than accepting responsibility because **Big Losers Always Make Excuses!** They criticize others and place **BLAME** in an attempt to rationalize their own shortcomings.

Do you think this "unique individual" might **BLAME** others for hiding his clothes? Or does it look like he is very proud to display some of his underlying gifts?

If we are transparent and honest might we need to accept the fact that others may criticize our actions? Can you accept criticism without placing **BLAME?** Can you tell the truth without placing **BLAME?** Is placing **BLAME** another form of lying? Is the risk worth the reward to be transparent?

Please write the words in order to spell the word BLAME.

Always	Losers	Excuses	Big	Make
_____	_____	_____	_____	_____

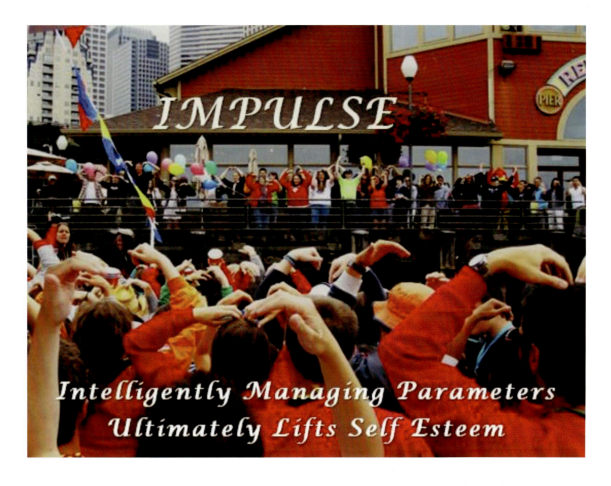

IMPULSE - Intelligently Managing Parameters Ultimately Lifts Self Esteem.

Can **IMPULSE** be a good thing? Certainly! Let's hope that our rapid reactions avoid infringing on the rights of others. There is certainly a fine line between good impulses and harmful impulses. Is this yet another indicator that we should be very careful of our actions and reactions?

If you were amidst a group of people who started singing "YMCA" would you impulsively join in? Can positive impulses bring us immeasurable joy?

Please write out the words to spell IMPULSE.

Esteem   Parameters   Intelligently   Lifts   Self   Managing   Ultimately

_____   _____   _____   _____   _____   _____   _____

Let's consider another definition of **IMPULSE**. Does this definition sometimes fit you?

Instantly Moving Parameters Usually Lowers Self Esteem. Do you think that many of the negative issues that you have created for yourself were done on an **IMPULSE?** Do you lower your feeling of self-respect when you make an inappropriate knee jerk reaction?

Would you like to be more cautious in allowing your future impulses? Are you involved in any addictions that began on an impulse? Do you know anyone who has a harmful addiction that began on an **IMPULSE** when somebody said… "go ahead and try this?"

Do we need to always consider the long-term consequences of our impulses?

Please write out the words to spell IMPULSE.

Parameters	Lowers	Esteem	Instantly	Usually	Self	Moving
_____	_____	_____	_____	_____	_____	_____

Please indicate your feelings in this survey regarding impulses by placing a "+" if you agree or a "—" if you disagree.

___ Impulses can be good impulses or bad impulses.

___ We should always be careful of how we respond with our impulses.

___ I have impulsively joined in singing, as an example at a birthday celebration.

___ Positive impulses can be very joyful; it's up to us to spread the joys.

___ I have done something impulsively that I later regretted.

___ An inappropriate impulse can lead to lowering self-respect.

___ I should always consider the consequences of my actions before I respond.

___ People are likely to make improper impulses if they are "under the influence."

___ I know someone who has an addiction that started on an impulse.

___ Everyone should be very cautious if someone says, "go ahead and try this!"

___ I just want instant gratification, I don't care about the consequences.

___ We should always consider the long-term consequences of our impulses.

___ "Think before you drink, chill before you pill, it's not a joke: never smoke."

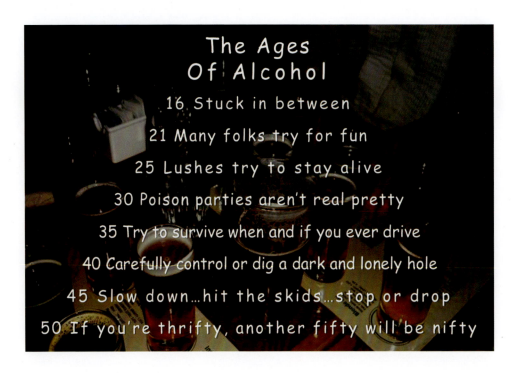

The Ages Of Alcohol…16 stuck in between…21 Many folks try for fun…25 Lushes try to stay alive…30 Poison parties aren't real pretty…35 Try to survive when and if you ever drive…40 Carefully control or dig a dark and lonely hole…45 Slow down…hit the skids…stop or drop…50 If you're thrifty, another fifty will be nifty!

Please place a number in each space to indicate how you feel about consuming alcohol.

1 = Never   2 = Sometimes   3 = Usually   4 = Mostly   5 = Always

____ I do not drink alcohol and I never plan to imbibe.

____ I am in control if I consume small amounts of alcohol.

____ I occasionally drink, but when I do, I usually get very intoxicated.

____ I drink almost every day, even though it bothers me.

____ I hide my drinking from others because I drink way too much.

____ My drinking causes problems with my finances, family and job.

____ I have zero control over alcohol, and I love getting intoxicated.

____ I feel that I am not able to remain sober if I start drinking.

____ I must prove my desire to stop drinking by seeking help.

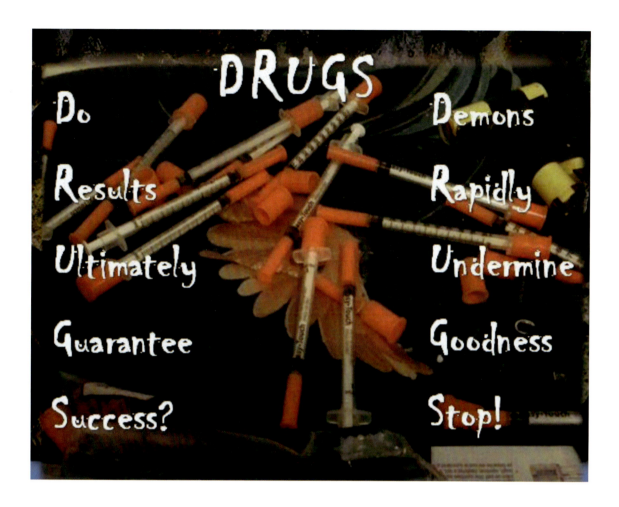

DRUGS - Do Results Ultimately Guarantee Success? Do you take prescription **DRUGS** to maximize your health? Synthetic **DRUGS** can be very beneficial in helping us lead healthy lives. As an example, guess who's recovering from his shoulder surgery? Hopefully you are not involved in too many prescription **DRUGS** or illicit substances that fit this definition of **DRUGS - Demons Rapidly Undermine Goodness Stop!**

You are probably aware that illicit drug involvement can lead to dependency that can create an avalanche of undesirable results. Do you know people who have been adversely affected by using illicit **DRUGS**? Have **DRUGS** created issues in your life? If you are involved with illicit **DRUGS**, would you like to stop before demons undermine your goodness?

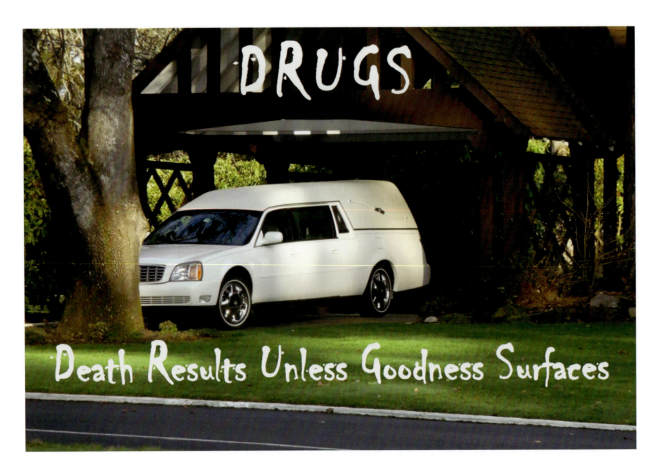

DRUGS – Death Results Unless Goodness Surfaces. The statistics for deaths due to using nicotine, alcohol, prescription **DRUGS** and illicit **DRUGS** are absolutely overwhelming. To prove this simply ask yourself if you know people who have died because they were involved with any of these chemicals.

Please write a "T" for True or "F" for False.

____ Nearly everyone knows someone who's died because of smoking, alcohol or **DRUGS**.
____ Almost everyone who experiences an illegal drug risks dying from their involvement.
____ The majority of people who go through drug and/or alcohol treatment relapse.
____ All humans are potentially at risk of becoming addicted to nicotine, alcohol or **DRUGS**.
____ Frequency of use + potency + heredity + painful events = possibility of addiction.
____ Almost all addicts and alcoholics continue using to avoid becoming physically ill.
____ The answers to the six questions above are true. (The answers in fact are true.)

Statistics from The National Institute on Drug Abuse report that over 2 million people in the United States visit hospital emergency rooms per year because of **DOPE - Demons Only Produce Evil**.

It is estimated that ten percent of Americans are involved with some form of **DOPE**.

Tens of thousands of people in the United States die each year due to **DOPE**.

More people succumb per year because of abusing **DOPE** than die in car accidents, murders or suicides.

Please place an "X" by the three statements that define DRUGS.

___ Do Results Ultimately Guarantee Success?

___ Demons Rapidly Undermine Goodness Stop!

___ Death Results Unless Goodness Surfaces!

___ Don't Restrict Use…Great Stuff!

___ Does Regular Use Generate Selfishness?

___ Delightful Reactions Unleash Gargantuan Sightings!

Saturates Most Organs…Kills Indiscriminately; Never Good - SMOKING.

People who smoke throughout their lives have a 50/50 chance of dying from a **SMOKING** related illness. Our mother passed away, at an early age, due to her lifetime of involvement with nicotine. We so wish that decades ago she would have said "NO SMOKING BEYOND THIS POINT." It was heart wrenching to witness her struggle to breathe while her lungs were rapidly losing their capacity to assimilate oxygen. Her early demise robbed our children of the opportunity to get to know and share their love with their grandmother.

If you smoke, can you stop? If you smoke, have you sought medical assistance to end your self-inflicted addiction? Please avoid leaving this earth in the horrific way my mother left her loving family!

Please define SMOKING by using the letters of the word.

Organs	Kills	Good	Never	Saturates	Indiscriminately	Most
_____	_____	_____	_____	_____	_____	_____

Please place an "X" by each ending you agree with for the following sentence.

"If I smoke or would ever begin smoking, the things that would probably help me stop smoking would be_____

__ setting a date to quit."
__ informing friends of my plans to quit."
__ keeping my plans to quit a secret."
__ replacing smoking with gum, candy, exercise."
__ staying away from occasions of temptations."
__ carrying a photo or souvenir in place of cigarettes."
__ writing down my feelings about quitting in a diary."
__ seeking help from medical professionals and my doctor."
__ discarding cigarettes, lighters, ashtrays, and matches."
__ visiting patients in a pulmonary ward."
__ hearing success stories from successful quitters."
__ making a list of people who don't want me to die."
__ rewarding myself with activities, hobbies and vacations."

Please place an "X" by all that apply to end the following sentence.

"My involvement in smoking is_____

____ nothing to worry about because I do not smoke nicotine products."
____ something I really enjoy, I see no reason to slow down or stop."
____ not healthy, I know that chewing and/or smoking can eventually kill me."
____ nobody else's business, people should not hassle me about smoking."
____ way out of control, it has created severe health problems for me."
____ horrible I wish I could stop, I have been unsuccessful in trying to stop."
____ not a good example for my friends and family to see."
____ impossible for me to stop, I know it will probably kill me!"

You will be more successful in eliminating undesirable habits if you pay close attention to your **TRIGGERS – Try Regulating Impulses; Good Guys Eventually Reject Stuff**. Have you analyzed why your peers might be pressuring you to begin or to continue undesirable habits?

Are your friends profiting by selling you something? Do they attempt to minimize their guilt by convincing you to be involved in drugs or alcohol? Are you living under their cloud of "misery loves company?" Have your friends become your enablers? Would your life be better if you reject some of your "so called…friends?"

Please indicate your opinion to the questions with a "T" for True and an "F" for False.

___ I have analyzed why my peers pressure me to begin or continue undesirable habits.

___ My friends are profiting by selling me products that are not good for me.

___ Friends attempt to minimize their guilt by trying to involve me in their bad habits.

___ Friends attempt to involve me in their bad habits because "misery loves company."

___ There are people in my life that perpetually enable my bad habits.

___ My life would be better if I would reject some of my "so called…friends."

___ I am going to begin eliminating people from my life who affect me in negative ways.

Imagine that you are an addict. Place an "X" by the following descriptions of situations to end the sentence that might "trigger" you to be involved with alcohol or drugs.

"It is very difficult for me to control my addiction(s)_____

___ if I frequent places where I used to be involved in alcoholic beverages and/or drugs."

___ if I am stressed, sick, celebrating, sad, mad, depressed, hung-over, upset or anxious."

___ because I need to be high to cope with any and all of my overwhelming problems."

___ so it is best for me to avoid them by developing new friends and new activities."

___ and it seems that after I get drunk or high my problems have usually gotten worse."

___ so I stay away from all people and places that might tempt me to begin again."

___ because people who don't care about me perpetually apply peer pressure."

___ because I know that I can resist absolutely anything except temptation!"

___ so I don't become physically sick from NOT being involved in drugs and/or alcohol."

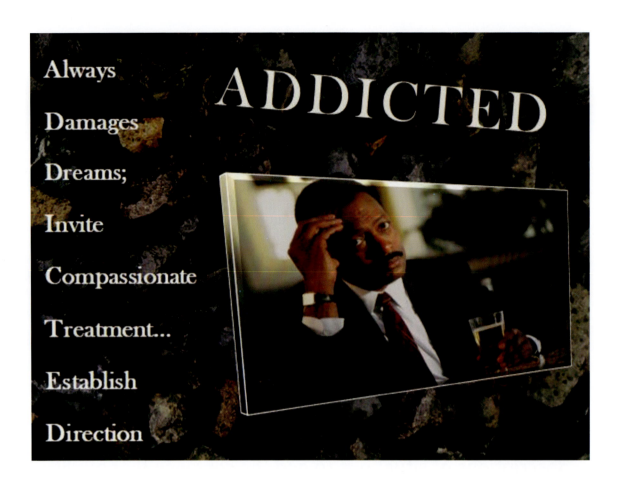

What is the term for people who are hooked on alcohol or drugs? **ADDICTED - Always Damages Dreams; Invite Compassionate Treatment…Establish Direction**. Do you have addictions that have shattered your goals and dreams?

If you have addictions would you like to establish a new direction rather than continuing the downward spiral of despair? If you are **ADDICTED**, for the love of your family and friends, please seek a new direction.

Please place an "X" by what can possibly be lost because of addictions.

____Self-respect	____Friends	____Job	____Joy
____Money	____Family	____Trust	____Dreams
____Physical health	____Freedom	____Happiness	____Love
____Hobbies	____Spiritualism	____Ambition	____Soul
____Home	____Desire to live	____Faith	____Hope
____Appearance	____Mental health	____Confidence	____Life

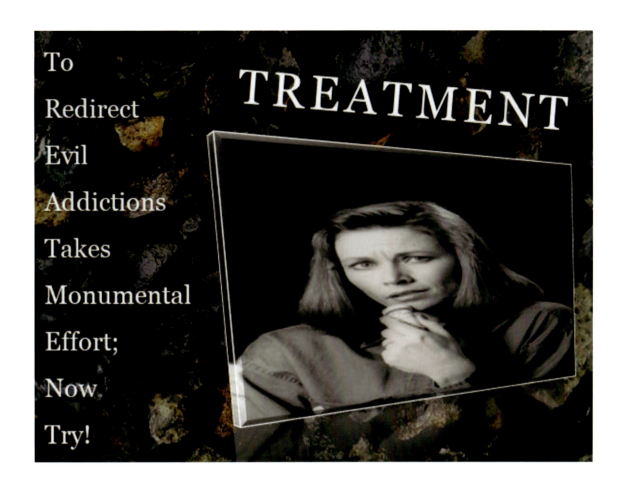

TREATMENT - To Redirect Evil Addictions Takes Monumental Effort; Now Try!
Let's take a look to see if you feel you are or are not… **ADDICTED – Always Damages Dreams; Invite Compassionate Treatment; Establish Direction!**

Please place an "X" by the statements that best describe you.

___ I am totally clean…I do not consume any alcohol or drugs.

___ Some of my friends and dreams have been lost because of my addiction.

___ Someday I will stop because I regularly imbibe more than I should.

___ I need help to stop my addiction, but I'm too embarrassed to admit I need help!

___ I am proceeding exactly in the direction of my dreams; I am really happy!

___ I am in pain. All I really care about is losing my problems in my addiction.

___ My dreams have been damaged. I need **TREATMENT**, I need a new direction.

___ I want to escape addition. It's up to me to **START – Success Takes A Realistic Try!**

When we hit rock bottom because of harmful habits we can easily feel locked away from family and friends. Harmful habits can result in burned bridges while we continue to imprison ourselves. These calamities are outcomes of developing habits that we **CRAVE - Conditioned Responses Always Victimize Everyone**.

Would you like to travel down your river of life without being imprisoned by something you **CRAVE?** If you have harmful habits would you like to avoid craving them? Here is a formula for avoiding what you might **CRAVE - Carefully Restricting All Vices Empowers!**

Please place a number on each space to help determine if you experience cravings.

1 = Nope   2 = Rarely   3 = Sometimes   4 = Usually   5 = All In

____ I have zero cravings for chemicals that might harm my mind and/or body.

____ I only do drugs or drink alcohol during the week or on weekends or both.

____ I only **CRAVE** harmful things during days of the week that end in d-a-y.

____ I **CRAVE** harmful substances every minute of every day.

____ I **CRAVE** to be free of cravings…I should seek help as soon as possible.

____ My cravings have convinced me that my body and mind need help.

____ I am going to seek help to reverse my physical and mental cravings.

____ I do not want to bother anybody with my addiction problems.

____ I am going to seek help today to try to eliminate my cravings!

____ I am ready to **START – Success Takes A Realistic Try.**

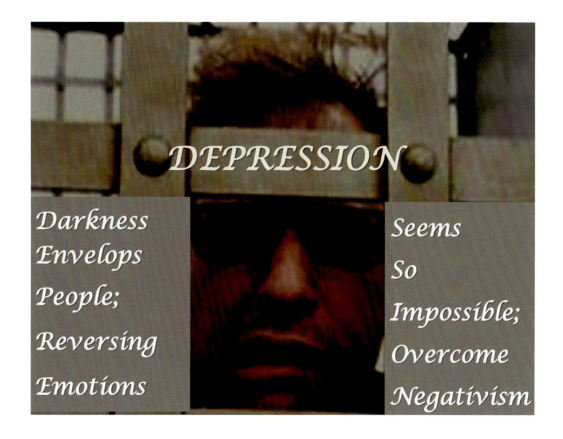

Cravings for unhealthy substances can take us to rock bottom and leave us imprisoned with overwhelming feelings of **DEPRESSION - Darkness Envelops People; Reversing Emotions Seems So Impossible; Overcome Negativism!** Alcohol and drug abuse lead to **DEPRESSION**…period. Our bodies and minds become addicted.

It takes a two-pronged approach of ridding our bodies and minds of the addictive substances. It takes physical and mental intervention to reverse the compounded **DEPRESSION** that can steal our soul. **DEPRESSION** can become a whirlpool sending us to a deep, dark hole that can be very difficult, if not impossible, to escape. Avoid substances, seek help, learn to enjoy all life has to offer!

Please place the words in the correct order to spell DEPRESSION.

| Reversing | Darkness | Negativism | So | Impossible |
| Overcome | Envelops | Emotions | People | Seems |

_____ _____ _____ _____ _____

_____ _____ _____ _____ _____

Have you been considering that you would like to have your habits proceed in a different **DIRECTION?** Are you **Deciding If Restructuring Everything Can Turn Issues Over Now?**

Are you in control of your life or have you lost your **DIRECTION?** Would you like to turn your life around? Easy to say…difficult to do, don't allow yourself to enter situations that are undesirable…change **DIRECTION!**

Place an "X" by the SINGLE most appropriate answer about the DIRECTION you are headed.

____ I am usually happy with my physical and mental habits.

____ I am unhappy with having to rely on substances to help me feel better.

____ I'm headed the wrong **DIRECTION** that will lead me to a disastrous dead end.

____ I am involved in too many harmful things that can potentially hurt me.

____ I can't imagine how I could be any happier with my life.

____ None of my habits are harmful…they are all just fun.

____ I need a new **DIRECTION**. My current habits will probably end up killing me.

Changing direction can consist of treating the physical dependency in addition to help with the mental complications through **THERAPY - Treasure How Experts Realign Anxieties Perplexing You!**

Hopefully you will take advantage of **THERAPY** if you are in need of conquering the overwhelming complications associated with escaping dependency.

Please place an "X" by everything on this list that you agree with.

___ **THERAPY** is for people who would like additional help with their personal challenges.

___ I certainly agree that effective **THERAPY** can be a very valuable experience.

___ Skipper provides his brand of **THERAPY** for the author of this material…here is a hint…yes!

___ I am going to prove I don't need **THERAPY** right now. I will eliminate my addiction.

___ I don't need **THERAPY** because there aren't any addictions affecting my life's balance.

___ People who love me suggest that I seek **THERAPY**. I will take their advice.

___ I am always willing to suggest **THERAPY** to anyone who might benefit from it.

___ My anxieties are affecting my life's balance. It's time for me to visit a therapist.

Have you ever hit absolute rock bottom? Have you ever felt like a total **REJECT - Restricting Evil Justifies Eliminating Certain Troubles?** Have you ever felt like "Chucky the Good Guy" from the movie "Child's Play?" Do you seem like a "Good Guy" until your evil traits surface and people try to **REJECT** you? Might it be time to change yourself if you have been rejected? If you have been rejected can you accept the fact that it is your fault and stop blaming others for your failings?

Please place a number 1-5 to express your opinion regarding rejection.

1 = Doesn't Apply   2 = Rarely   3 = Maybe   4 = Usually   5 = I Agree

___ My relationships are stable; I am not concerned about being rejected.

___ I am going to **REJECT** people who have been my enablers.

___ I know someone who's been rejected because of their addiction.

___ Rejection can be a useful step to help point out an addiction issue.

___ It is ridiculous to **REJECT** someone because of their addiction.

___ People with addiction need love and treatment not rejection!

___ Rejection can be a wakeup call that can potentially save many lives.

___ My addiction is not my fault. People should not **REJECT** me.

___ I have been rejected. I am going to seek help with my addiction!

"Sometimes your measure of friendship isn't your ability to not harm…but your capacity to forgive the things done to you…and ask forgiveness for your own mistakes." This John Maxwell quote points out that everyone occasionally offends others. The key is having the capacity to forgive and to ask for forgiveness is paramount for creating peace of mind. Asking for forgiveness can be very difficult, however extremely rewarding. To help eliminate walls and find peace of mind is there anyone you would like to ask for forgiveness?

Even if someone fails to offer you forgiveness, will you feel better because you gave forgiveness a try? Do you listen to people offering you forgiveness and do you do your best to accept sincere forgiveness to tear down walls and build bridges?

Please respond to each statement with a "Yes" or "No."

_____ Asking for forgiveness can be very difficult, however extremely beneficial.

_____ I would like to be forgiven for something I did wrong when I was younger.

_____ Asking for forgiveness usually helps me feel better, even if not accepted.

_____ I will tell someone I expect them to apologize to me if they have offended me.

_____ I have an open mind about giving people an opportunity to offer me forgiveness.

_____ To help tear down walls and build bridges I am open to accept a sincere apology.

Please place an "X" by the three statements that comprise John Maxwell's quote regarding the importance of forgiveness.

___ "Sometimes your measure of friendship isn't your ability to not harm

___ it is the other person's fault, don't worry about it

___ granting forgiveness is a sign of personal weakness

___ friends are not important, they just cause drama

___ but your capacity to forgive the things done to you

___ and ask forgiveness for your own mistakes."

___ keeping your walls up minimizes the pain you feel from others.

Fairly Offering Reconciliation Grants Inspiration; Vendetta Erased

Are you hoping that people will **FORGIVE** you? **Fairly Offering Reconciliation Grants Inspiration; Vendetta Erased.** Letting go of past problems with others is a major step towards developing peace of mind. Learning how to seek forgiveness and asking for atonement for past discrepancies helps us put the past behind and move on with our lives. Helping others overcome barriers builds trust and respect.

Can you **FORGIVE** yourself? Can you **FORGIVE** others? Can you ask for forgiveness today?

Please write in numbers 1-4 to spell the word FORGIVE.

___ Inspiration;

___ Fairly Offering

___ Vendetta Erased

___ Reconciliation Grants

Does a new dawn encourage you to have **FAITH?** Ideally the new day helps you **Forget All Insecurities Trust Hope!** Do the lights turn on in your life to give you hope? Can you forget your fears and move forward? Do you concentrate on the light or do you concentrate on the darkness? Do you choose to fear the future because of your past failures? Or are you inspired to apply your positive attitude to allow you to have faith in your future?

Please spell the word FAITH by writing the words in order.

Hope	Trust	Forget	Insecurities	All
_____	_____	_____	_____	_____

Please place an "X" by the statements you agree with.

___ I have **FAITH** that a new day turns the lights on in my life to give me hope.
___ Even though it's difficult, I am trying to forget my fears and move forward.
___ I try to focus on the positive things that bring light, rather than the negative things.
___ I will receive instant gratification by perpetually reminding myself of my **FAITH**.
___ I have too many past problems, I know my problems will be the same in the future.
___ I have **FAITH** in the future, even though I have some fear of repeating the past.
___ I firmly believe that it's "HOW HIGH WE BOUNCE THAT COUNTS!!"

Ideally your faith fills you with **HOPE - Harnessing Optimism Produces Empowerment**. It is certainly beneficial to have faith that provides us **HOPE**, however it is up to us to get "tooled up" and go "Get-R-Done." Does your faith inspire you to enact **HOPE** to help you reach unimaginable heights? Are you willing to take the steps to put your **HOPE** into reaching your goals? Are you harnessing your energies in the right direction or blaming others for your shortcomings? It's nice to say, "just do it" …but it's really nice to say… "just did it!"

Please spell the word HOPE by writing the words in order.

Empowerment   Optimism   Harnessing   Produces

_____ _____ _____ _____

Please place an "X" by the statements you agree with.

___ Stuff just happens to me, I have absolutely no control over anything in my life.

___ Faith is a farce, there is no reason to have **HOPE**, I'll never be able to change anything.

___ I always look for ways to improve and apply effective **TOOLS - To Optimize Our Lives**.

___ I am proud to say I am making improvements in my life.

___ I have faith that I can enact my hope to continue reaching towards my goals.

___ I have **HOPE** in taking my next **STEP- Start To Eliminate Procrastination**.

___ I am practicing my faith and **HOPE** by working through the steps to reach my goals.

Hopefully you can **Just Open Your Soul** so your **SOUL** can become your **Source Of Unconditional Love** allowing you to share yourself with others so you can **Just Offer Your Spirit**. Many think this simple formula for life develops a balanced existence leading to fulfillment.

Are there any steps you would like to take to nourish your **SOUL?** Will you allow that nourishment to permeate your **SOUL?** Will you open the door for goodness to enter? Are there many people you would like to share your **JOYS** with? Is there a reason you are waiting to share your **JOYS**?

Please place an "X" by the statements you agree with.

____ I have decided I will (or will continue to) be very organized to nourish my soul.

____ I will surrender my **SOUL** to accept what I need to change to reach my goals.

____ I will constantly search for positive goodness and reject anything that might harm me.

____ I will give back by sharing my gifts and talents to help others any way possible.

____ I will not allow myself to have an **"SDD"**; I refuse to have the **"Some Day Disease."**

____ I will keep very busy with self-help activities, helping others and pursuing my hobbies.

____ I will help myself and others avoid harmful habits by always enacting this definition of **TODAY - Triumph Over Demons Afflicting You!**

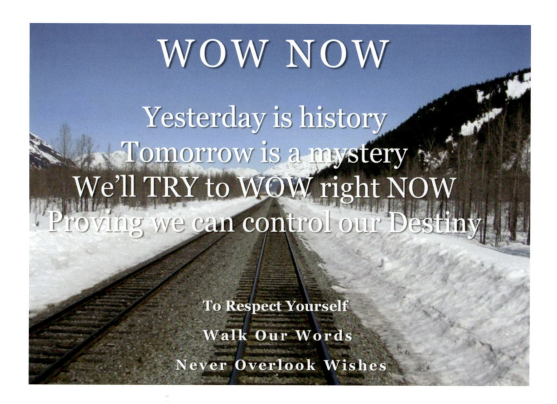

You will have benefited from this experience if you can **WOW NOW**…Yesterday is history, Tomorrow is a mystery, We'll **TRY** to **WOW** right **NOW** Proving we can control our destiny! If you understand…**To Respect Yourself…Walk Our Words… Never Overlook Wishes**.

I sincerely hope this experience has helped you understand the dangers of addiction and will help you "stay on track" with your desire to avoid any future chemical dependencies! Please prove you have discovered the silver bullet; **DESIRE - Ditching Evil Stuff Is Required Everyday!**

Please define the following words with their acronyms.

JOYS_____

SOUL_____

JOYS_____

TRY_____

WOW_____

NOW_____

DESIRE_____

87

When you reflect on this material, I hope this statement encapsulates your feelings; "The true test of our value is how we value ourselves."

This quote took us a long time to develop, I hope it resonates with you for the rest of your life!

Please place an "X" by the words that describe you.

__conversationalist	__entertainer	__caregiver	__counselor
__storyteller	__reader	__helper	__learner
__friend	__housekeeper	__hard worker	__listener
__smiler	__giver	__confidant	__improver
__handyman	__gardener	__fixer	__builder
__mediator	__musician	__collector	__provider
__cook	__comforter	__hugger	__self-starter
__music lover	__sports fan	__gamer	__athlete
__organizer	__babysitter	__forgiver	__bridge builder

Would you like this to be your "Personal Mission?" Yes___   No___

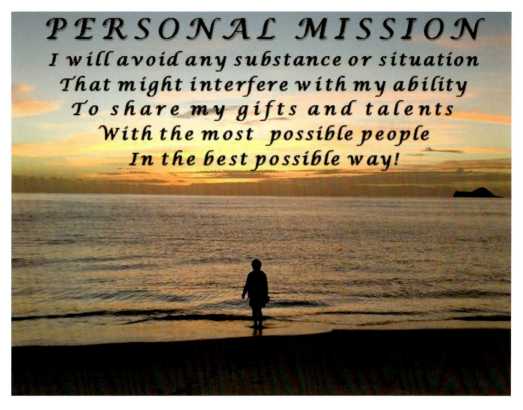

Ask yourself if "His Pillow" describes your feelings about departing this life.

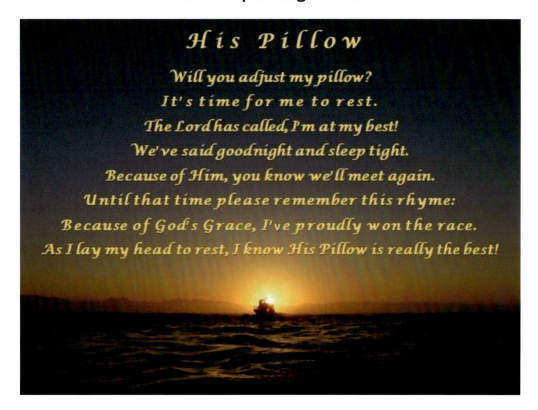

GOALSSSS

Goodness Only Awaits Labor - Start, Sweat, Sustain, Succeed!

List two goals and assign numbers 0 to 10 (10 being high) to each consideration of the goals-setting process.

GOALSSSS * * * *

	(First Goal)	(Second Goal)
1. Level of need/passion	_____	_____
2. Level of desire to sacrifice	_____	_____
3. Level of research/planning	_____	_____
4. Level of organization/action	_____	_____
5. Ability to accept change	_____	_____
6. Ability to endure criticism	_____	_____
7. Available resources/assistance	_____	_____
8. Available time/energy	_____	_____
9. History of patience	_____	_____
10. History of commitment	_____	_____
Probability Index Total	_____	_____

Probability Index Scoring

90–100…Celebrate Success!

80–89…Go for it!

70–79…Do you have a CANDO ATTITUDE?

60–69…Do you have the DESIRE to CHANGE?

50–59…Will you work hard to CHANGE?

40–49…Do you need to develop your DESIRE?

30–39…Do you want to be stuck in old HABITS?

20–29…Are you near rock bottom?

10–19…Have you hit rock bottom?

0–9…Hopefully you want to live; get help!

TODAY'S DESIRES
Triumph Over Demons Afflicting You…Ditching Evil Stuff Is Required Everyday
Please place an "X" under Yes or No for each sentence.

		Yes	No
1.	I desire to keep all my bad habits, all my friends and lifestyle.		
2.	I desire to admit that I need to be responsible for my actions.		
3.	I desire to have the nerve to admit what I need to change.		
4.	I desire to take the actions it will take to change my bad habits.		
5.	I desire to avoid anxiety, shame, blame, pain, lying and dying.		
6.	I desire to be organized and be responsible for my well-being.		
7.	I desire to avoid mood swings, needless anger and withdrawals.		
8.	I desire to avoid being physically ill or mentally incapacitated.		
9.	I desire to be involved in healthy activities with caring friends.		
10.	I desire to eat properly, get enough sleep and exercise regularly.		
11.	I desire to have help identifying and overcoming my problems.		
12.	I desire to turn my problems into challenges and fix them.		
13.	I desire to let go of the past and pursue plans for my future.		
14.	I desire to seek forgiveness from people I may have offended.		
15.	I desire to possess enough resources to live comfortably.		
16.	I desire to be loved by the people I hope to have love me.		
17.	I desire to use common sense to help me abide by all laws.		
18.	I desire to avoid negativism, punishment and incarceration.		
19.	I desire to avoid grudges, guilt, depression, self-harm and suicide.		
20.	I desire to have honest role models mentor me to be my best.		
21.	I desire to be an inspirational role model for others to follow.		
22.	I desire to respect myself by constantly improving my life.		
23.	I desire to have people respect and admire my improvement.		
24.	I desire to be happy by living a sober life free from all addiction.		
25.	I desire to help others, giving my life a direction and purpose.		
26.	I desire to **DESIRE – Ditching Evil Stuff Is Required Everyday.**		
27.	I desire to start* changing my habits to enjoy a balanced life.		
28.	I desire to sweat* while working towards my best life possible.		
29.	I desire to sustain* my happiness by displaying my commitment.		
30.	I desire to struggle **TODAY** for everything it takes to succeed*.		

ACTION PLAN

Please place an "X" by all that apply.

To improve the balance in my life, I will need to:
___ Be responsible for my own actions, accept change and take actions to improve.
___ Be responsible for my own actions, accept change and take actions to improve.
___ Be responsible for my own actions, accept change and take actions to improve.
___ Be responsible for my own actions, accept change and take actions to improve.

**Please place an "X" by the actions you plan
to take and then complete the sentences.**

_____ I will seek help from the following individuals:
_____
_____
_____
_____

_____ I will seek help from the following organizations:
_____
_____
_____
_____

_____ I will need to accept the following things I cannot change:
_____
_____
_____
_____

_____ I will not associate with the following people:
_____
_____
_____
_____

____ I will not allow this list of emotions and situations to trigger my addiction(s):

_____
_____
_____
_____

____ I will avoid the following mind-altering chemicals:

_____
_____
_____
_____

____ I will avoid the following situations that tempt me to practice risky behaviors:

_____
_____
_____
_____

_____ I will forgive myself and ask the following people to forgive me for my past actions:

_____
_____
_____
_____

____ I will ask forgiveness for the following things that I have done:

_____
_____
_____
_____

_____ I will attempt to improve the balance in my life by learning how to:

_____
_____
_____
_____

_____ I will seek inspiration from the following sources:

_____
_____
_____
_____

_____ I will enjoy the following hobbies and activities:

_____
_____
_____
_____

_____ I will help the following people improve their lives by:

_____
_____
_____
_____

_____ This is a partial list of people who do not want to see me die:

_____
_____
_____
_____

PROPOSED OBITUARY

Please fill this out as you hope it will appear after you leave this life...

(Name)_____ was born in (place)_____

on (date)_____ to (parents)_____

Attended schools at _____

and developed the following skills_____

(First name) _____ helped others by _____

_____

There will be a celebration of life at (place)_____

We will be praising our friend for overcoming struggles with:

_____

_____

We will be praising our friend for accomplishing the following things:

_____

_____

(First name) _____ enjoyed the following hobbies and activities:

_____

_____

We hope that our loving friend and family member has been a role model for everyone to always do the following positive things:

_____

_____

We hope that our loving friend and family member has been a role model for everyone to always avoid the following things:

_____

_____

Our loved one will always be remembered for:

_____

_____

_____

_____

HOOKED CROSSWORD

Character Construction Company

ACROSS

4 Fabulous Relationships Inspire Empathy Not Drama
7 Always Limit Consumption Often Hinders Our Lives
9 Just Offer Your Spirit
12 Demons Rapidly Undermine Goodness; Stop
14 Celebrate Life Escape Addictions Now
15 Triumph Over Demons Afflicting You
17 Always Damages Dreams Invite Compassionate Treatment Establish Direction
19 To Respect Yourself
20 Didn't Realize Until Now Klunk
24 Demons Only Produce Evil
25 Individuals Need Support Philosophically In Reaching Expectations
28 Staying Off Booze Eliminates Remorse
29 Instantly Moving Parameters Usually Lowers Self Esteem
31 Saturates Most Organs Kills Indiscriminately; Never Good
34 Regain Essential Control Over Vices; Everyone Respects You
35 Activating Meaningful Beliefs Is The Inspiration Often Needed
38 Never Overlook Wishes
40 Ditching Evil Stuff Is Required Everyday
42 Start To Eliminate Procrastination
46 Losers Intentionally Exaggerate; Stop
48 Darkness Envelops People, Reversing Emotions Seems So Impossible; Overcome Negativism
50 Harmful Actions Blatantly Injure The Soul
51 Some Day Disease
52 To Redirect Evil Addictions Takes Monumental Effort; Now Try
55 Restricting Evil Justifies Eliminating Certain Troubles
57 Just Open Your Soul
60 Be Ambitious And Accountable
61 To Optimize Our Lives
63 Intelligently Managing Parameters Ultimately Lifts Self Esteem

DOWN

1 Death Results Unless Goodness Surfaces
2 Didn't Even Notice I Always Lie
3 Bountiful Love Endures Scorn'n Sadness; Enters the Deity
5 Control All Negativism; Develop Optimism
6 Fairly Offering Reconciliation Grants Inspiration; Vendetta Erased
8 Losing Every Temptation Generates Opportunities
10 Powerful Resources Await Your Every Request
11 Boundaries And Limits Are Necessary; Careful Everybody
13 Forget All Insecurities Trust Hope
15 Try Regulating Impulses, Good Guys Eventually Reject Stuff
16 Forget Overeating Observe Diet
18 Certain Habits Always Negatively Ground Everyone
20 Do Results Ultimately Guarantee Success
21 Correct Habits Activate New Goals Effectively
22 Deciding If Restructuring Everything Can Turn Issues Over Now
23 Happiness Advances By Isolating Temptations
26 Carefully Restricting All Vices Empowers
27 Great Opportunity
30 Managing Our Victimization Effectively Overcoming Neglect
32 Habitual Overuse Often Kills Escape Dependency
33 Managing Our Outlook Daily
36 Nice Opportunity
37 Conditioned Responses Always Victimize Everyone
39 Walk Our Words
41 Exercising My Personal Actions To Help You
43 Pages Always Stay Turned
44 Big Losers Always Make Excuses
45 Success Often Requires Rescinding Yourself
47 Success Takes A Realistic Try
49 Put Away Sorrowful Things
53 Always Trying To Improve Takes Unswerving Dedication Everyday
54 Treasure How Experts Realign Anxieties Perplexing You
56 Change Addictions To Ambitions Let Yourself Succeed Today
58 Source Of Unconditional Love
59 Clean And Sober Habits
62 Harnessing Optimism Produces Empowerment

HOOKED WORD SEARCH

After you have circled all the listed words,
then circle the individual letters that spell the acronym for TRY.

```
T O A R E S P E H O P E C T T N E M T A E R T
Y O F T I U R S S T A R T E L F N R W V B Q T
T X A N T M Y G N I K O M S X M E R V X Y S Q
N H I Q M I P A M B I T I O N C L L B L Y M N
K W T K G N T U K P T Y V N O M O L T L Y O R
H G H H K W K U L Z P R H V L H A R A N E B F
D R U N K D X V D S Q T E Q O M F T D V N S Y
C T K T E C N D D E E R B C E O A E O N G T L
Y L V T P C P E J M Y D L T O C K M J U W P P
R W S H O E L Z I T R A M D Q O G O R N N C R
R Q R R D R R E R R Y E M L O L Y D J Z M W A
O V V G E N E I A K F D M H J S C S D R F S Y
S T J L B G S B S N D E L P O C K R E D N T E
M M C T A G G T O E Z T V V A D J Q V I C I R
R D I H L M P I E S D C N M T T N T T X L B M
L O N E A M H A R P Z I Q N M Z H A D F Q A K
G O S R N V S C S T N D R T N J N Y C X M H D
T M P A C C A V B T B D O G T E L N L T G E L
Y J I P E M C Y R W R A D R C Q R L O D N U D
C H R Y R N X C H A N G E W R G R D X I O V M
L G E E V I G R O F T D O L A N A X A S P L N
N O I S S E R P E D T W D Y V Y T L J K L N N
L B K W G F D E S S E L B K E R Z N O W M M Z
```

Character Construction Company

ADDICTED	CHANGE	FAITH	LETGO	SORRY
ALCOHOL	CLEAN	FOOD	LIES	SOUL
AMBITION	CRAVE	FORGIVE	MOOD	START
ATTITUDE	DENIAL	FRIEND	MOVEON	STEP
BALANCE	DEPRESSION	HABITS	NOW	THERAPY
BLAME	DESIRE	HOOKED	PAST	TODAY
BLESSED	DOPE	HOPE	PRAYER	TREATMENT
CANDO	DRUGS	IMPULSE	RECOVERY	TRIGGERS
CASH	DRUNK	INSPIRE	SMOKING	TRY
CATALYST	EMPATHY	JOYS	SOBER	WOW

TERM	PAGE	DESCRIPTION
ADDICTED	15, 74, 75	Always Damages Dreams Invite Compassionate Treatment Establish Direction
ALCOHOL	22	Always Limit Consumption; Often Hinders Our Lives
AMBITION	52	Activating Meaningful Beliefs Is the Inspiration Often Needed
ATTITUDE	36	Always Trying To Improve Takes Unswerving Dedication Everyday
BAAA	52	Be Ambitious And Accountable
BALANCE	14, 30	Boundaries And Limits Are Necessary; Careful Everybody
BLAME	62	Big Losers Always Make Excuses
BLESSED	44	Bountiful Love Endures Scorn'n Sadness; Enters the Deity
CANDO	14	Control All Negativism Develop Optimism
CASH	24	Clean And Sober Habits
CATALYST	51	Change Addictions To Ambitions Let Yourself Succeed Today
CHANGE	28, 47, 48	Certain Habits Always Negatively Ground Everyone
CHANGE	29	Correct Habits Activate New Goals Effectively
CLEAN	20	Celebrate Life; Escape Addictions Now
CRAVE	76	Carefully Restricting All Vices Empowers
CRAVE	76	Conditioned Responses Always Victimize Everyone
DENIAL	60	Didn't Even Notice I Always Lie
DEPRESSION	77	Darkness Envelops People Reversing Emotions Seems So Impossible; Overcome Negativism
DESIRE	13, 14, 15, 87, 91	Ditching Evil Stuff Is Required Everyday
DIRECTION	78	Deciding If Restructuring Everything Can Turn Issues Over Now
DOPE	69	Demons Only Produce Evil
DRUGS	67, 69	Demons Rapidly Undermine Goodness; Stop
DRUGS	67, 69	Do Results Ultimately Guarantee Success
DRUGS	68, 69	Death Results Unless Goodness Surfaces
DRUNK	23	Didn't Realize Until Now…Klunk!
EMPATHY	34	Exercising My Personal Actions To Help You
FAITH	14, 84	Forget All Insecurities; Trust Hope
FOOD	25	Forget Overeating Observe Diet
FORGIVE	83	Fairly Offering Reconciliation Grants Inspiration; Vendetta Erased
FRIEND	32	Fabulous Relationships Inspire Empathy Not Drama
GO	21	Great Opportunity
HABITS	25	Harmful Actions Blatantly Injure The Soul
HABITS	26	Happiness Advances By Isolating Temptations
HOOKED	2, 4	Habitual Overuse Often Kills; Escape Dependency
HOPE	14, 85	Harnessing Optimism Produces Empowerment

TERM	PAGE	DESCRIPTION
IMPULSE	63	Intelligently Managing Parameters Ultimately Lifts Self Esteem
IMPULSE	64	Instantly Moving Parameters Usually Lowers Self Esteem
INSPIRE	37	Individuals Need Support Philosophically In Reaching Expectations
JOYS	86, 87	Just Offer Your Spirit
JOYS	86, 87	Just Open Your Soul
LET GO	47, 48	Losing Every Temptation Generates Opportunities
LIES	59	Losers Intentionally Exaggerate; Stop
MOOD	14	Managing Our Outlook Daily
MOVE ON	49, 50, 59	Managing Our Victimization Effectively; Overcoming Neglect
NEW DAY	36	Now Enjoy Wishes Decisions Affect You
NO	21	Nice Opportunity
NOW	87	Never Overlook Wishes
PAST	14, 19	Put Away Sorrowful Things
PAST	18	Pages Always Stay Turned
PRAYER	46	Powerful Resources Await Your Every Request
RECOVERY	15, 16	when you…Regain Essential Control Over Vices; Everyone Respects You
REJECT	80	Restricting Evil Justifies Eliminating Certain Troubles
SDD	86	Some Day Disease
SMOKING	70	Saturates Most Organs; Kills Indiscriminately; Never Good
SOBER	22	Staying Off Booze Eliminates Remorse
SORRY	55	Success Often Requires Rescinding Yourself
SOUL	86, 87	Source Of Unconditional Love
START	53, 75, 76	Success Takes A Realistic Try
STEP	39, 52, 85	Start To Eliminate Procrastination
THERAPY	79	Treasure How Experts Realign Anxieties Perplexing You
TODAY	86, 91	Triumph Over Demons Afflicting You
TOOLS	43, 85	To Optimize Our Lives
TREATMENT	75	To Redirect Evil Addictions Takes Monumental Effort; Now Try
TRIGGERS	72	Try Regulating Impulses; Good Guys Eventually Reject Stuff
TRY	54, 87	To Respect Yourself
WOW	87	Walk Our Words

SOURCES OF INFORMATION

Communication FOCUS
http://characterconstructioncompany.com/Content/Default.aspx

National Survey on Drug Abuse
https://nsduhweb.rti.org/respweb/homepage.cfm

National Institute on Drug Abuse
https://www.drugabuse.gov/

Drug Facts: Understanding Drug Abuse and Addiction
https://www.drugabuse.gov/.../drug facts

Bureau of Justice Statistics
http://www.bjs.gov/

Substance Abuse and Mental Health Services Administration
http://www.samhsa.gov/

National Intervention Referral Service
http://nationalinterventionreferral.org/

24/7/365 CONTACTS IN USA FOR IMMEDIATE HELP

Emergency   911
Recovery Helpline 866 789 1511
Substance Abuse and Mental Health National Hotline   800 662 HELP (4357)
National Poison Control Hotline   800 222 1222
National Suicide Hotline   800 273 TALK (8255)
Substance and Mental Health Services Administration   800 662 HELP (4357)
National Alcohol Hotline   800 331 2900
National Drug and Alcohol Abuse Hotline   888 506 0699

THE PROFESSOR, SKIPPER AND MARY ANN

Mr. Brummond developed his successful character-building tools and techniques while serving as a music educator, school district administrator, organizational trainer, public speaker and instructor in jails and prisons.

Mrs. Brummond added her expertise with her knowledge of human interaction acquired during her career serving as a college administrator.

The Character Construction Company team is indebted to the addicts, law enforcement personnel, mental health professionals, medical professionals and addiction therapists who have assisted in developing HOOKED to help people work towards living a balanced life free from addiction.

Additional Character Construction Company Courses

1. CHANGE
2. HONESTY
3. ATTITUDE
4. RESPECT
5. ACHIEVEMENT
6. CHOICES
7. TRUST
8. EMPOWERMENT
9. RELATIONSHIPS
10. INSPIRE
11. SELF-WORTH
12. TEAMWORK
13. INTEGRITY
14. COMMUNICATION
15. SUCCESS
16. BULLY

Courses available at www.LearningCharacter.com